Getting Started in

VALUE
INVESTING

The *Getting Started In* Series

Getting Started in

VALUE INVESTING

Charles S. Mizrahi

BICENTENNIAL
1807
WILEY
2007
BICENTENNIAL

John Wiley & Sons, Inc.

Published by John Wiley & Sons, Inc., Hoboken, New Jersey.
Published simultaneously in Canada.
Wiley Bicentennial Logo: Richard J. Pacifico

For general information on our other products and services or for technical support, please contact our
Customer Care Department within the United States at (800) 762-2974, outside the United States at
(317) 572-3993 or fax (317) 572-4002.

Wiley also publishes its books in a variety of electronic formats. Some content that appears in print may not
be available in electronic books. For more information about Wiley products, visit our web site at
www.wiley.com.

Library of Congress Cataloging-in-Publication Data:
Mizrahi, Charles, 1962–
    Getting started in value investing / Charles Mizrahi.
        p. cm. – (The getting started in series)
    Includes bibliographical references (p.   ) and index.
    ISBN 978-0-470-13908-0 (pbk.)
    1. Stocks   2. Value investing   I. Title.
    HG4661.M567 2008
    332.63'22–dc22   2007013690

Printed in the United States of America

10   9   8   7   6   5   4   3   2   1

Contents

Chapter 7

Chapter 8

Chapter 9

Chapter 10

Chapter 11

Acknowledgments

I am grateful to my friends and colleagues for their careful reading of the manuscript. Their critiques greatly improved the content. I am especially indebted to Raymond A. Gindi, Ira L. Horowitz, and Dr. Cesar "Bud" Labitan. Dr. John Price greatly shaped my thinking on how to determine intrinsic value and the importance of factoring in a margin of safety.

Words of encouragement and support—offered to me by two people I have the highest respect for, Donald Yacktman and Rabbi Joseph Telushkin—came at a time they were needed most.

I would like to thank my editor at John Wiley & Sons, Debra Englander, for agreeing to publish my manuscript and guiding me through every step of the publishing process. Michael C. Thomsett, an author of over 60 books, provided me guidance, suggestions, and his vast expertise. I was fortunate to have such a capable team behind me.

I owe an enormous debt of gratitude to Warren E. Buffett. Like his teacher Benjamin Graham before him, Mr. Buffett has continued the tradition of passing on an investment philosophy to all those who will listen. His life is an example of what happens when wisdom, ethics, and benevolence converge.

In addition to allowing me to marry their only daughter (for which they have my eternal gratitude), my in-laws, Richard and Sallie Mishaan, have been a constant source of encouragement and inspiration.

While growing up, my parents, Billy and Janice Mizrahi, provided me with an environment that allowed me to develop my love of learning and reading. They gave my brothers and me total freedom to find our own way in life while gently guiding us from the wings. I hope I can have the same faith in my children that they had in us.

For over a quarter century, my brother Gary Mizrahi has been my partner, confidant, most outspoken critic, and friend. The great businessman William Wrigley once said, "When two men in a business always agree, one of them is unnecessary." Our relationship is one in which we bring our own viewpoints and strengths to the table, and it has made working together both a challenging and a rewarding journey.

I have been blessed with the greatest children a father could ask for: Janice, Billy, Ritchie, Jeffrey, and Steven. I pray that you always keep in mind "what the Lord requires of you: only to do justice, and to love goodness and to walk modestly with your God, then will your name achieve wisdom" (Micah 6:8).

I owe the deepest gratitude of all to my wife Ellen, a true woman of valor. "Many women have done well, but you surpass them all" (Proverbs 31:29).

I couldn't agree more with Sir Isaac Newton, who said, "If I have been able to see further, it was only because I stood on the shoulders of giants." I have been very fortunate to be able to learn so much from so many. It is now my turn to pass it on.

Getting Started in
VALUE
INVESTING

Value Really Means Something

I have seen no trend toward value investing in the 35 years I have practiced it. There seems to be some perverse human characteristic that likes to make easy things difficult.[1]

—Warren Buffett

" I just don't have a head for investing, don't waste your time," my mother told me. It was a cool fall afternoon and already starting to get dark when Mom and I were sharing a pot of herbal tea. My mother always avoided the subject like the plague because to her investing and everything related to it was one big black hole. It was a place where information was likely to be siphoned away and never seen again. I couldn't blame her. Since I was a teenager, she had always seen me with either a book in my hand or leafing through a company's latest annual report—scribbling down notes and calculating numbers. Dad had always taken care of the family finances and still did. But I felt strongly that Mom should have some idea of how to manage money too.

After my further pleading, she told me that I could have two minutes; if she couldn't grasp it by then, it would be the last she wanted to hear on the subject. Sitting at the kitchen table, I knew this was the only chance I would get and I couldn't blow it. "Mom, how much do you pay for a half gallon of milk?"

Without hesitating for a nanosecond she replied, "$1.49." If she went to the supermarket and milk was selling at $4.99, would she buy it? "Are you crazy, not a chance," was her answer. How about if the same milk was selling at another supermarket for $0.79, would she buy it? "In a heartbeat, I would probably buy three," she beamed.

"Mom," I said, "you just described the essence of value investing: Make a purchase only when you get more value for your money, or keep walking. The rest is commentary."

The Miracle of Turning Clear Water into Mud

Wall Street has a way of making something simple seem extremely complex. Like the Wizard of Oz, Wall Street has done a terrific job complicating, confusing, and intimidating, so that people with average intelligence feel rather stupid. Many times Wall Street does one thing and tells investors to do the exact opposite especially when it comes to investing their nest eggs in mutual funds. A mutual fund's marketing department preaches buying shares and holding them for decades, yet the portfolio managers of those very same funds hold them in the portfolio only an average of nine months.

Getting Started in Value Investing cuts through all the obstacles that have been placed in your path for making sound investment decisions. After reading this book, you will have a firm grasp on how to make an informed decision on what types of stocks to buy, and, more importantly, what to avoid. You will also have a solid foundation with an approach that has worked on Wall Street for the past 70 years. How well you do will depend on how successful you are at keeping your emotions in check and avoiding the latest fads on Wall Street.

The Stock Market at the Turn of the Twentieth Century

One hundred years ago, there was no effective regulation in the stock market. So insider trading and even outright manipulation were commonplace and the average person was at a clear disadvantage. Until 1910, the New York Stock Exchange (NYSE) reserved a special "unlisted department" for companies that did not even disclose *any* financial information. By 1926, nine out of 10 NYSE firms submitted some form of financial audit, but this was not required until the FDR-era reforms of 1933 and 1934. Many so-called preferred list securities were sold privately even before shares were offered (at higher prices, of course) to the general public. During the abuses of the 1920s, no fewer than 100 NYSE-listed stocks had prices fixed, and nothing seemed to effectively remedy these problems.[2]

With scant accurate financial information, investors bought and sold stocks based on Ouija boards and superstition. J.P. Morgan, the most powerful banker and financier in the early 1900s, was known to have said that "millionaires don't use astrology, billionaires do."

During this time, investors were groping for anything that could help them predict the future direction of stock prices. At the turn of the twentieth century W.D. Gann, known to his followers as the founding father of financial astrology, believed that specific geometric patterns and angles had unique characteristics and that these could be used to predict price movements. In 1934 the Dow Theory, which was based on trends in price for the Dow Jones Industrial and Transportation Average, was gaining a wide following. In 1938, Ralph Nelson Elliott developed the Elliott Wave Theory, which said that the stock market trades in repetitive cycles, which could be divided into patterns he termed "waves." Trend lines, price patterns, astrology, and waves were just a few of the ways investors used to predict price movements; I kid you not. A different way of looking at the market was still some years away.

> *"Thousands of experts study overbought indicators, oversold indicators, head-and-shoulder patterns, put-call ratios, the Fed's policy on money supply, foreign investment, the movement of the constellations through the heavens, and the moss on oak trees, and they can't predict markets with any useful consistency, any more than the gizzard squeezers could tell the Roman emperors when the Huns would attack."[3]*
> *—Peter Lynch*

Dawn of a New Way of Thinking

At the age of twenty, Benjamin Graham graduated from Columbia University in 1914 and was asked to join the faculty of three departments—English, philosophy, and mathematics. Instead, Graham went to make his fortune on Wall Street starting as an analyst, and then managing an investment partnership. In 1934, Benjamin Graham and coauthor David Dodd wrote the book *Security Analysis* in which they laid out the intellectual framework for what was later called value investing; this book was geared to the professional investor. This work was like a ray of sunshine peeking through the clouds of confusion. In 1949 Graham followed up with *The Intelligent Investor*, a version of his earlier book but this time aimed to the individual investor.

Graham's approach to analyzing a stock could be boiled down to three major points:

1. Think like a business owner. When making an investment in a stock, keep in mind you are buying a part of a business.
2. The stock market is there to serve you, not instruct you. Most of the time, the stock market prices businesses correctly. However, there are times when the stock market greatly overvalues or undervalues businesses.
3. Make a purchase only when there is a gap between the stock price and the underlying value of the business. The wider the gap the more "margin of safety" you have.

Throughout this book, you will meet some of the investors who learned at the feet of Graham as a teacher and/or employer. Each one attributes their success to the philosophy laid out by Graham more than 70 years ago and has the track record and net worth to prove it works.

Old Habits Die Hard

Many studies and papers have been written over the past several decades on how value investing works. In later chapters, I summarize a few landmark studies that make the point. None of this, however, has stopped academics from trying to prove that the market is efficient and there is no way that an investor can beat the market. For example in the 1970s the Efficient Market Theory (EMT) became quite popular in the halls of academia. In a nutshell, EMT says that all market participants receive and act on all information as soon as it sees the light of day. Those who follow this theory believe that there is perfect information in the stock market. As soon as information becomes available about a stock, everyone has it at the same time, and the price of the stock should reflect the knowledge and expectations of all investors.

In other words, don't waste your time analyzing companies; it will do you no good. How do proponents of EMT invest their own money? Since making stock selections in order to outperform the stock market is futile, they buy a stock index fund and are happy to match the stock market's return. The main flaw in this theory is that it neglects to take into account the number one reason the stock market becomes inefficient at valuing companies: human emotion. When it comes to money, most people hate losing. During periods of panic, investors won't pick up $1 bills selling for 50 cents with a 10-foot pole. Efficient markets become very inefficient when fear grips Wall Street. Business schools continue to teach EMT and as a value investor, you should be glad. Warren Buffett took a positive view regarding EMT and wrote:

> In any sort of a contest—financial, mental, or physical—it's an enormous advantage to have opponents who have been taught that it's useless to even try. From a selfish point of view, Grahamites should probably endow chairs to ensure the perpetual teaching of EMT.[4]

What You Find in This Book

I have written this book for the average person who wants to develop an understanding of what value investing is all about. Once you have finished this book, you will be among a select group of investors able to view the stock market and all the noise that surrounds it with more clarity and peace of mind.

Chapter 1 explores the most common misconceptions investors have about value investing and explains why they don't work in the real world. In Chapter 2, I take you through the basics and provide you with the compelling logic of value investing. Here you will see why this is the only approach that has withstood the test of time.

Following these basics, Chapter 3 gives you a framework for investing in stocks, and even shows you why putting all of your eggs in *one* basket simply makes sense and improves your overall return. Chapter 4 examines another important concept, which is finding businesses that truly are the champs. In Chapter 5, I explain the importance of picking not only great businesses but great managers as well, which is another way of adding value. Chapter 6 explains the importance of competition and why certain companies invariably have a strong competitive advantage.

Chapters 7 and 8 give you sound nontechnical explanations of a company's financial statements, how to read them, and what you need to make value-based interpretations. In Chapter 9, I tie up the whole concept by explaining how *price* and *value* differ, and how to determine exactly what you should pay for a stock. Chapter 10 is devoted to reminding you about some of the mistakes people make in the way they invest, and why, as a value investor, you actually simplify your decision-making process by sticking to a short list of tried-and-true ideas. I provide you with some final thoughts in Chapter 11.

Words to Live By

Warren Buffett has often said that intelligence is no guarantee for success when it comes to investing. He has observed that anything above a 125 IQ is wasted.

You certainly don't have to be the smartest kid in the class to apply a value approach to investing. And if you were never good at math or do not have a head for numbers, so what? That will probably be an advantage since you won't be bogged down in detailed analysis. You will be better able to focus on what makes your portfolio tick: the business (stock) you are buying. Instead of spending hours looking at the cash flow statement, you will be asking yourself relevant questions like: What edge does this business have? Is management candid? In other words, the qualitative stuff that is not so readily found in the numbers.

Your present occupation should not be a barrier, either. Great value investors come from all walks of life: a lawyer (Charlie Munger), IBM salesman (Rick Guerin), chemistry major (Tom Knapp), advertising executive (Stan Perlmeter), high school graduate (Walter Schloss). Most people get the concept of value investing in five minutes or less, and that's the point: It isn't complex or overly technical. You can do it.

> *"It is extraordinary to me that the idea of buying dollar bills for 40 cents takes immediately with people or it doesn't take at all."*[5]
> —*Warren Buffett*

So turn the page and let's begin.

The 5 Misconceptions of Value Investing

We've long felt that the only value of stock forecasters is to make fortune tellers look good. Even now, Charlie and I continue to believe that short-term market forecasts are poison and should be kept locked up in a safe place, away from children and also from grown-ups who behave in the market like children.[1]

—Warren Buffett

Whenever I go to a dinner party or social gathering, a friend or acquaintance usually asks my opinion on the economic news flash of the day. For example, if the media are talking about the DJIA making an all-time high or an unemployment report coming in better than expected, people who know that I manage a limited partnership and write an investment newsletter want to hear my take on current economic events. I usually respond the same way each time I am asked: "I really don't have a clue how it will affect the stock market or the economy." I'm not trying to brush them off, but I really don't know. In fact, I don't even take those factors into account when making a purchase.

> **DJIA**
> An index of 30 stocks traded on the public exchanges. It is the most widely known index and is used as a measure of the health and direction of the overall stock market.

value investing
a method of determining the value of a business and then buying shares at a discount from that value.

top-down approach
a method of identifying investment opportunities by making a prediction about the future, determining the investment consequence, and then selecting the proper security.

bottom-up approach
a method of identifying investment opportunities one at a time through analysis of financial statements and the outlook of the company.

Top-Down Approach vs. Bottom-Up Approach

Because I follow a *value investing* philosophy, I have the advantage of taking a *bottom-up approach*, which means identifying investment opportunities one at a time through analysis of financial statements. In contrast, most professional investors take a *top-down approach*, which carries with it greater risk of being wrong. Let's look at the way the top-down and bottom-up approaches differ, and you decide which approach carries with it a higher degree of uncertainty.

Top-Down Approach

The largest 100 *money managers* hold $6.8 trillion of stocks or 52 percent of the U.S. stock market's total market capitalization. Eighteen managers each supervise more than $100 billion of U.S. equities, including four managers who each hold some $400 billion or more.[2]

A large percentage of these money managers employ a top-down approach when making an investment in stocks. This involves three steps:

1. Making a prediction about the future.
2. Discerning its effect on the investment.
3. Making the trade.

This approach is a very risky way to go because each step of the way is subject to error. Money managers who take this path are basically making a big picture or macro bet on the future. Once they pass that hurdle, they are faced with interpreting the impact of their decision on the sector, industry, and then company in order to maximize the value of their prediction. If that weren't hard enough, they then

TABLE 1.1 Top-Down Approach Exercise	
1. Big-picture prediction	A weak U.S. economy
2. Conclusion drawn from prediction	Value of U.S. dollar should decline
3. Areas of investment	U.S. companies—large exposure to foreign currency
4. Specific investments	Coca-Cola, IBM, Pfizer, and so on.
5. Timing	Need to purchase ahead of crowd

have to act quickly before the rest of Wall Street makes the same trade, causing prices to rise and minimizing any profit potential they would have had.

Now consider an example of all the steps that a top-down investor has to get right to make a profitable decision. Table 1.1 shows how a weak U.S. economy has to be called right.

The top-down investor is faced with many un-knowns, and also has to play beat the clock. For example, even if the top-down investor is correct on the big-picture prediction, the conclusion from that prediction and the area of investment (i.e., a weak U.S. economy will cause the dollar to decline, making companies that have large foreign-currency exposure show higher earnings because of currency gains), they can still drop the ball and pick the wrong specific investment (bought Coca-Cola instead of IBM) and even lose money on the trade. Then they have to make the correct specific investment (i.e., Coca-Cola, IBM, Pfizer, etc.) ahead of the other thousands of money managers who are all looking at the same big-picture prediction.

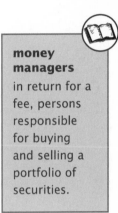

money managers in return for a fee, persons responsible for buying and selling a portfolio of securities.

When they are buying the specific investment, what kind of margin of safety will they have? They are buying based not on value but on which company, regardless of stock price, will move higher the fastest. And one last hurdle: Top-down investors have to know when the trend has run its course. How much of the recent stock move is already factored into the price? For me, the top down approach is fraught with risks each step of the game and does not offer any margin of safety that would satisfy me.

Bottom-Up Approach

The bottom-up approach used by investors employing a value investing philos-ophy is much easier to execute and doesn't require making predictions of events that are unknowable. Bottom-up investors look at stocks one at a time and use good, old-fashioned analysis such as reading the company's *annual report* and *SEC Form 10-K*s. After evaluating the company and determining an appropriate price to pay (which includes a margin of safety), they then check the price the stock is trading.

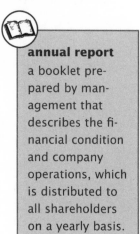

annual report
a booklet prepared by management that describes the financial condition and company operations, which is distributed to all shareholders on a yearly basis.

SEC Form 10-K
audited report filed annually with the Securities and Exchange Commission. Similar to the shareholder annual report but provides more detailed financial and nonfinancial information.

If the stock is currently trading below the price they used to determine the underlying worth of the business, they will buy the stock and wait patiently for it to rise. That's it. In the short term, it really doesn't matter much what the economy, the stock market, or the U.S. dollar will do, as long as the bottom-up investor was able to buy $1 worth of value for 70¢. In other words, this whole approach can be described as "buy it cheap and forget it."

The hard part for bottom-up investors is the lack of activity; but keep in mind, the market rewards patience. It could take months or even years for the stock market to reward you for your patience. But if you have the correct temperament and are not swayed by the daily gyrations of the stock market, you will be rewarded when the underlying value of the business catches up with the price you paid for the stock.

If you act as a bottom-up investor, the unknown factors are mostly within your control. You only have to be right regarding the valuation of the company at the time you bought the stock. If you take the time to figure out the underlying worth of the business and make sure there is a wide gap between valuation and price (the wider the gap, the greater the margin of safety), you will be able to figure out the potential risk and reward on your investment.

For example, if your analysis concludes that Coca-Cola is worth $50 a share, and the stock is currently trading at $35 per share, or 30 percent lower than the current price, you already know you have the potential to make a 43 percent on your investment. Even if you are wrong on the valuation and it really should have been valued at $45 a share, (or $10 higher than your initial valuation), you can still walk away with a 29 percent return. (Value is $45; you buy it at $35: The difference of $10 is a 29 percent profit.)

The Easier Game

The examples just mentioned make the point and tell you which approach allows you to sleep better at night. When you follow a bottom-up approach, the chance for errors and mistakes along the way will be much lower than the chance of trying to predict the future of the U.S. economy or what inflation will be over the next five years. Legendary fund manager Peter Lynch offered very sound advice about making predictions:

> Nobody can predict interest rates, the future direction of the economy, or the stock market. Dismiss all such forecasts and concentrate on what's actually happening to the companies in which you've invested.[3]

It's much easier to stick to what you can know rather than trying to figure out the unknowable.

The biggest problem I see for top-down investors is in determining when the investment no longer makes sense or simply knowing when they are wrong. They also have to speculate on the magnitude of their prediction. If they predict that the U.S. dollar will fall, they then have to predict by how much so they can capitalize on their prediction.

That is something the bottom-up investor doesn't have to waste time worrying about. If the company undergoes new management, or a supplier or sales channel suddenly closes up, the bottom-up investor would then be able to assess and reevaluate the situation. For top-down investors, there is no clear answer; the best they can do is to make a judgment call. Judgment calls made in the heat of the moment are usually wrong. In addition to the logic and simple steps used by a bottom-up investor, I promise you will sleep better at night. And to me, that is worth all the tea in China.

Common Misconceptions about Value Investing

Before we go on, I want to take a moment and share with you five of the most common misconceptions people have about applying a value approach to stock investing. Value investors do not let others make up their mind for them; they absorb the facts and then come to a decision. Independent thinking is a trademark of value investors. Benjamin Graham said: "If you formed a conclusion from the facts and if you know your judgment is sound, act on it—even

Profile: Warren Buffett

With net worth of approximately $52 billion, Buffett is the second-richest person in the world (after Microsoft founder Bill Gates) and is arguably the greatest investor of the past century. The Oracle of Omaha is CEO and the largest shareholder of Berkshire Hathaway. He graduated from the Wharton School and the University of Nebraska, with a master's from Columbia Business School. Among his accomplishments, Buffett earned the only A+ grade ever given by Benjamin Graham in his security analysis class.

Buffett purchases businesses that he can understand, has competent management in place, has an enduring competitive advantage, and will purchase them only at an attractive price. From 1965 to 2006 Berkshire Hathaway grew at an average annual return of 21.4 percent while the S&P 500 index gained 10.4 percent. A $10,000 investment in Berkshire Hathaway in 1965 would now be worth $36 million.

Securities and Exchange Commission (SEC)

the federal agency responsible for oversight of publicly listed corporations, and for enforcing laws and regulations at the federal level.

though others may hesitate or differ. You're neither right nor wrong because the crowd disagrees with you. You are right because your data and reasoning are right.[4]

1. *Much of the information needed to research a stock is too costly, hard to get and difficult to understand.* I am not a big fan of any government agency but I do have to take my hat off to the Securities and Exchange Commission (SEC). Many of the SEC statutes are designed to promote full public disclosure and protect investors from fraud. Because of the SEC, there is an enormous amount of information that publicly traded companies need to disclose.

Most if not all of your research can be had by reading a company's annual report. At the end of a company's fiscal year they send out to all shareholders a report informing them how the company did the past year, what they are planning to do, and the challenges the company will face. The letter is written by the chairman of the board or CEO. Once you get past the charts, graphs, and glossy pictures of smiling employees, you find a wealth of financial information tucked away in the back of the report. This is where you can find the real meat and potatoes of how the company is doing.

Many successful investors recommend you read the past four to five years of a company's annual report as part of your research. You will then be able to see if they kept promises made in previous years, admit to mistakes, and have a consistent message. In other words, since you are a shareholder, you are the real owner of the company and the annual report is the company's way of reporting back to you how well they've done over the past year.

Most annual reports are written in a very friendly and relaxed manner and are not difficult to understand. The great part about annual reports is that they are free. All you need to do is call the company and request it or go to their web site and download or read it. A large percentage of your research can be found by just reading the annual reports. You will be amazed at how few investors read them. In addition to calling the company, there are many free sites on the Web that not only have financial data on a company, but with one click you can compare how a company is performing against its competitors. Today, in only a few hours you can learn more about a company from the comfort of your favorite arm chair that only a decade ago would've cost you thousand of dollars and have taken weeks to gather. Thank the SEC and the Internet for helping create a level playing field for investors allowing them to access information for no cost.

2. *You can't beat the stock market.* Like everything else in life, this statement is both a reality and misconception for different types of investors. If you love hearing hot tips from your doorman who has a son who has a friend who works in the mailroom of ACME Industries, and is certain that they are coming out with a product that will set the world on fire, you don't stand a chance of beating the market. After hearing some analyst from Big Brokerage, Inc. talk up 5 different stocks in fewer than 30 seconds and you can't wait to buy them all, you will have a slim chance of outperforming a money market fund, and you can forget about outperforming the stock market.

If, however, you begin to view stocks as pieces of businesses, purchase quality companies when they are selling for fair prices, ignore the daily gyrations of the stock market, and hold stocks for the long term, then you have a very good chance of beating the market. Fortunes have been made by investors with modest means, who bought quality companies and held on to them for years. Imagine you have invested $1,000 and have divided it equally among the following three companies: Procter & Gamble (makers of Crest toothpaste and dozens of other consumer products), McDonald's (home of the Big Mac), and Pepsico, (maker of Pepsi, Mountain Dew, and other beverage and snack products) on the last day of 1976.

You picked these three companies because they have been in business for years, are market leaders, and you are very familiar with their products. Right

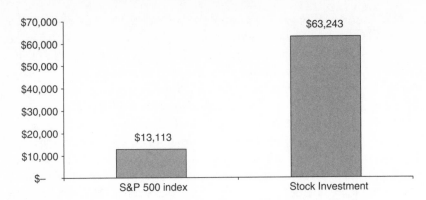

FIGURE 1.1 Results If You Invested $1,000 among Procter & Gamble, McDonald's, and Pepsico on 12/31/76, and Held Them for 30 Years.

after you buy shares in these three companies, you go on a 30-year mission for NASA to explore the planet Saturn and will not be able to change your stock positions or find out how the companies are doing for the next three decades. Upon arriving back on Earth on the last day of 2006, you open up your brokerage statement to find out that your $1,000 is now worth $63,000, easily outperforming the S&P 500 index, which would have grown to only $13,000. You were amply rewarded for investing in companies that you understood and held for the long term, while ignoring the stock market. You can beat the market if you stick to a few of the principles I share with you in this book. See Figure 1.1.

3. *Value investing is all about buying stocks trading at low prices.* Trying to determine if a stock is selling at a good value based on a single number is a mistake most investors and professionals have in common. That's almost like being asked to determine if someone is over or under weight without ever seeing or knowing anything about them. If I told you that my friend Joe weighs 200 pounds and asked you to tell me if he is over or underweight, you would probably ask me a few questions about him. You might ask his age, height, body frame, occupation, how often he exercises, and so on. If you found out that Joe is six feet tall and plays tight end for the New York Jets, you would say he is underweight (average weight for tight ends 2006 NFL draft: 257 lbs.).[5] On the other hand if I told you Joe plays center field for the Boston Red Sox you might conclude that he is the proper weight for his position.

If you try to buy a stock based on the level of the stock price, most likely you will be buying a lot of terrible companies and you will be missing out on great ones. Berkshire Hathaway Class A (BRKA) shares trade at about $108,000 per share, the most expensive shares traded on U.S. stock exchanges. Yet there are many excellent value investors who are scooping up shares at this price because they determined that the shares are cheap and are really worth between $125,000 and $150,000 per share. According to them, the stock price is not properly valuing the earnings of the company and the stock is trading at a discount to its underlying value.

On the flip side, Bombay Company's (BBA) stock at $1.00 per share may be too high a price for this ailing furniture retailer. Soft sales, terrible earnings, and immense competition might force this company to close its doors as it recently needed to borrow money to pay bills. Simply because it is trading at a low price doesn't make it a value investment. A value investor is never concerned with the price level of a stock. As you have seen, a company can be a great value at $108,000 per share and a terrible value at $1.00. The price of the stock always has to be measured against the worth of the underlying business. It doesn't matter what price the stock is trading for as long as you are getting more in value than what you paid for the stock.

4. *You have to be an accountant to understand a company's financial statements.* If you are the type of investor who buys a stock simply because it is going up or it's in a high flying industry, odds are you never even looked at a company's financial statement. I would wager that most investors who bought stocks in the past decade looked only at the pictures in the company's annual report and never looked at the financials. That should give you some idea as to the advantage you have if you educate yourself to a few simple accounting concepts.

If you have no idea how to read a financial statement, you are not alone. Many business executives I've met have no clue, either. By not knowing basic accounting you will have a very difficult time valuing a business. Accounting is the music of business and by learning how to hum just a few simple tunes, you will avoid overpaying for quality companies and can achieve a higher return on your investments.

It helps to know something about accounting to be a value investor but if you don't, have no fear. If you can figure out how much you made if you bought something for $10 and sold it for $15 and incurred $2 of expenses, you will do alright (a profit of $3).

Most investors don't even bother looking at a company's financial statements because they were never taught what to look for. Thanks once again to the SEC, there are four statements that public companies need to file each quarter: balance sheet, income statement, cash flow statement, and statement of change in stockholder's equity. These statements give you a snapshot of the company's health. Why four and not one statement? Because four statements allow you to come to a conclusion on the health of the company from four different vantage points. Picture going to a doctor to have your heart checked. The doctor might take your blood pressure, do an EKG. and order a blood workup so that he or she can get a complete rundown on your heart. Each test provides the doctor with valuable information so he or she can make a proper diagnosis.

Financial statements provide that same view to the investor on a company's financial health. A balance sheet shows the financial position (assets, liabilities, and net worth) of a company as of a specific date in time. The income statement shows how much money came in (sales or revenue) and how much was paid out (expenses) for a period of time, usually a full year or quarter. By subtracting the money that came in from the money paid out, you arrive at the amount the company put into its pocket (net profit). The cash flow statement shows where the money came from and where it was spent for that same period of time. And the statement of change in shareholders' equity reports tells you the change in shareholder equity for a certain period of time (you don't need to deal too much with this statement). You certainly don't have to be an accountant to be a value investor and once I show you what to look for on the financial statement, it will be a piece of cake.

    5. *You can make more money investing in growth stocks than value stocks.* Should stock investors favor "value" stocks or "growth" stocks? This argument always strikes me as silly. Isn't every investment about value—buying something below its underlying value? Should we classify someone who buys an item at a price that is greatly above its underlying value a growth investor? The basic difference I see is value investors buy growth companies, too, but they don't want to pay top dollar for them. They take a more conservative and cautious view of the future. On the other hand, growth investors pay up for growth in anticipation that it will continue. Their read of the future is usually more optimistic than value investors'.

Investors have been conditioned to believe (assisted by Wall Street's marketing machine) that investing for growth is the converse of investing for value. Charlie Munger, vice chairman of Berkshire Hathaway, had this to say about this foolish argument: "The whole concept of dividing it up into 'value' and 'growth' strikes me as twaddle. It's convenient for a bunch of pension fund consultants to get fees prattling about and a way for one adviser to distinguish himself from another. But to me, all intelligent investing is value investing."[6]

I couldn't agree more. The goal of investing should be to buy businesses that are selling below their underlying value. A stock market investor should look at the profit margins, operating incomes, and return on equity of a business, regardless of whether it is labeled a "value" or a "growth" stock, and then factor in future earnings growth to determine whether the stock is undervalued or overvalued. If there is a wide gap between your valuation of the business and the value the stock market is giving it, you should buy. That's basically it; value investors try to get more value for their money.

Warren Buffett said: "The two approaches are joined at the hip: growth is always a component in the calculation of value. As long as you are buying great companies for less than their real worth, don't give a darn as to what investing style it is called, just watch your account balance rise over time."[8]

My purpose in this chapter has been to show how the bottom-up and top-down approaches work and why the bottom-up approach makes more sense and carries with it less uncertainty. Forget about trying to predict the future growth of the economy or where interest rates are headed; no one can do that. Instead, spend your time finding good

Profile: Charles Munger

A graduate of Harvard Law School, Munger was given some solid advice by Warren Buffett, who said, "Law was fine as a hobby but he could do better."[7] A few years later, Munger left his law firm and started investing. Today he works with Buffett as vice chairman of Berkshire Hathaway. His net worth is about $1.6 billion.

He guided Buffett from a pure Graham style of investing, which only looked at the financials of a company, to focus more on the quality of the business. Buffett gives him the credit for much of the enormous success of Berkshire Hathaway.

Munger is a worthwhile model for how value investing can work. First, he limits his investments to businesses with a sustainable competitive advantage; he buys them at a fair price; and finally, he believes that a portfolio of three companies is plenty of diversification. Munger is content to invest a lot of capital in very few holdings and hold those positions for a long time.

His extreme patience combined with extreme decisiveness has paid off handsomely. From 1962 to 1975, Munger's partnership returned a compound annual return of 13.7 percent, after fees, versus 5.0 percent for the Dow Jones Industrial Average. During that time, a $100,000 investment in the partnership would have grown to $530,745 versus $188,565 if it had been invested in the Dow Jones Industrial Average.

businesses selling at attractive prices. By the time you finish this book, you will have all the tools you need to find them.

In the next chapter I show you why value investing is the most logical approach to take when investing in the stock market and how academics still don't get it.

Key Points

1. Bottom-up investing makes more sense than top-down investing. It places unknown factors within your control.

2. Independent thinking is a trademark of value investment, as exemplified by Warren Buffett, today's best-known and greatest value investor.

3. The goal of investing should be to buy businesses that are selling below their underlying value.

Chapter 2

The Basics of Value Investing: A Few Things You Must Know

There are two questions that I hear every time investors pay silly prices that have no relationship to the underlying value of a company: Does value investing work and will it continue to work regardless of what you might hear in the popular media? I would like to tell you about a conversation I overheard several years ago.

During the height of the stock market bubble in 2000, I attended an investment conference and overheard two money managers discussing how each viewed himself as an investor. I don't recall what they said to each other, but I do remember how they ended the conversation. I heard one say to the other, "Yeah, value is really out of style and probably will stay that way for a long time."

At the time, I recall thinking how silly that statement was—and still is. How could value investing be out of style? Isn't the objective of every investment to buy something at below its intrinsic value and sell it above that purchase price? If someone offered you a five-story brownstone on Fifth Avenue in New York City for $1 million, wouldn't you buy it in a heartbeat? You really don't need to know much about real estate to know that would be a great deal. Basically, you'd be buying an asset that is priced materially lower than the market price in anticipation of making a profit when you sell it.

Charlie Munger, vice chairman of Berkshire Hathaway, said at a Berkshire Hathaway shareholder meeting in 2000, "All intelligent investing is value investing—to acquire more than you are paying for." The compelling logic of this simple statement speaks volumes to me. A research paper titled *Searching for Rational Investors in a Perfect Storm* by Louis Lowenstein[1] should once and for all dispel the nonsense that the stock market is always efficient.

Efficient Market Theory

Many forests have been laid to waste by the number of research papers that academics have written over the past decades on *efficient market theory (EMT)*. The theory is relatively simple: In order to make money in the stock market, investors have to compete with so-called smart money investors, rational investors who are constantly searching the market for opportunities. Because of the smart money, all new information is already reflected in the market, so there's no point in scouring over company reports or financial statements. The smart money has already erased any discrepancy between price and value. You could do just as well having monkeys throw darts at the stock tables in the newspaper.

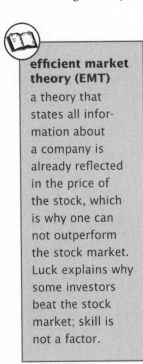

efficient market theory (EMT)
a theory that states all information about a company is already reflected in the price of the stock, which is why one can not outperform the stock market. Luck explains why some investors beat the stock market; skill is not a factor.

For years the academic world has paid homage to this great theory, and I doubt you can find more than a handful of professors who will tell you otherwise. Not only is it taught by academics to thousands of business students every year, it has also gained a following from business managers and professional money managers as well. The theory is based on a belief that markets are efficient all of the time. Despite market events (like the October 1987 crash and dot.com bubble of 2000), which demonstrated that the market can become inefficient, academics continue to cling to this broken theory. Warren Buffett said: "Apparently, a reluctance to recant, and thereby to demystify the priesthood, is not limited to theologians."[2]

EMT contends that if you just read that Wrigley, coming out with a new flavor of chewing gum, expected to increase earnings, should you buy the stock? Forget it, that information is already priced into the stock by the "smart money" investors. Sorry, pal, you're too late to the party. How, then, can an investor make money in the stock market if there's really no beating the smart money? The answer is easy: Buy a well-diversified index fund such as the S&P 500. You will at least match the market and save the trading costs and hours spent researching.

Lowenstein then goes to work to show how the EMT cannot in fact be relied upon, using the dot-com bubble to illustrate his point. In the late 1990s, stock prices became so detached from value that the market exceeded even the 1920s in its wild excesses. In a very short span of time, the NASDAQ rose from 1,200 (April 1997) to 5,000 (March 2000), for a gain of 316 percent, before plummeting back down to 1,100 (October 2002), for a loss of 78 percent. The rise and subsequent fall of the NASDAQ occurred over a five-year span. Where were all the smart money investors during that period? How did they allow the market to spin out of control? Did the smart money investors lose money during this period as well?

The Really Smart Money

Since no one can really identify the so-called smart money investors to see how they did during the selling frenzy, are there any rational investors who did not suffer the losses that so many other investors suffered? If so, what did they do right? The answer is, yes, there is a group of investors who did very well during the deflating of the bubble. It so happens that they share a common philosophy called value investing. Their results are amazing: Value investors beat the market averages by huge amounts, hold concentrated portfolios (a small number of securities), and hold stocks for years.

In his paper, Lowenstein selected 10 "true blue" value funds to see how they did in the five-year boom-to-crash period from 1999 to 2003. The funds he studied were the following:

1. Clipper Fund.
2. FPA Capital.
3. First Eagle Global.
4. Longleaf Partners.
5. Legg Mason Value.
6. Mutual Beacon.
7. Oak Value.
8. Oakmark Select.
9. Source Capital.
10. Tweedy Brown American Value.

Did these funds follow the crowd? Did the portfolio managers stick to their principles? Did the funds avoid the meltdown? The findings should have big implications for investors, traders, and academics.

The portfolio managers of these funds all have one thing in common: They attribute their strategy to a book published more than 70 years ago by Benjamin Graham and David Dodd called *Security Analysis.* Typically, these managers search for companies that are trading at a substantial discount from the value a reasonable buyer would pay for the business as a whole. They also factor in a "margin of safety" to allow for the inevitable risks of trying to project future earnings and cash flow. Warren Buffett explained a margin of safety by saying,

> If you understood a business perfectly and the future of the business, you would need very little in the way of a margin of safety. So, the more vulnerable the business is, assuming you still want to invest in it, the larger margin of safety you'd need. If you're driving a truck across a bridge that says it holds 10,000 pounds and you've got a 9,800 pound vehicle, if the bridge is 6 inches above the crevice it covers, you may feel okay, but if it's over the Grand Canyon, you may feel you want a little larger margin of safety. . . .[3]

Following the Crowd

Lowenstein's first test was to see if these funds followed the crowd and were sucked into the mania along with everyone else. His basis for comparison was an article in the August 2000 issue of *Fortune.* The editors of *Fortune* had selected stocks with very high profiles and had penned an article called "10 Stocks to Last the Decade." The subtitle of the article was "Here's a buy-and-forget portfolio." The 10 stocks were:

1. Broadcom.
2. Charles Schwab.
3. Enron.
4. Genetech.
5. Morgan Stanley.
6. Nokia.
7. Nortel Networks.
8. Oracle.
9. Univision.
10. Viacom.

At the time, these stocks had an aggregate market cap of more than $1 *trillion.* They were the must-haves of the new economy and had very high P/E ratios (only one was less than 50). By the end of 2002, these 10 stocks had declined an average of 80 percent from the July 2000 prices quoted in the article.

With the exception of Legg Mason Value, which had purchased Nokia in 1996 and had sold it in mid-2000 for a 1,900 percent gain, and Mutual Beacon, which had short positions (betting that the stocks would fall) in Viacom and Nortel, none of the 10 value mutual funds from Lowenstein's study included any of the stocks mentioned in the *Fortune* 2000 article. Why didn't these value funds join the fun and buy any of the *Fortune* 10? A sample of responses from the fund managers echoed consistent themes: "We did not buy Enron. . . . [we] could not understand its financial statements," said one. "Ridiculous valuations," said another. "Faulty disclosure, and we didn't like management," said yet another. Most of the other managers gave the traditional Graham–Dodd response: "Price relative to value was not attractive."[4]

Sticking to Their Principles

The stock market bubble did not peak until March 2000. By that time most, if not all, of these value funds were sorely out of tune, trailing the S&P 500 and the NASDAQ in 1999. Even though they were in danger of losing substantial assets under management as investors chased performance elsewhere, the fund managers continued to reaffirm the underlying investment principles, never lowering the funds' standards. In other words, they stuck to their guns. In 1999, with money flowing to technology, telecom, and Internet stocks that were trading at gravity-defying multiples, value managers were scooping up so-called old-economy stocks that were selling at substantial discounts to intrinsic value.

Avoiding the Meltdown

The value managers knew that all they had to do was wait it out and prices would once again make sense. After all, "history has proven that, over time, stock prices, although volatile in the short term, will converge with intrinsic business value."[5] If one assumes that there is no rhyme or reason why stocks move higher or lower (the *random walk theory*), one would expect half of the funds to have better performance than the index and the other half to have worse performance than the index, for a 50/50 split. But that's not what happened.

The return of the 10 value funds was staggering. Each and every fund outperformed the S&P 500 index by a huge amount. Mathematicians call this a five-sigma event, or one that cannot be explained by pure chance. The five-year average annual return through

random walk theory

a theory that stock prices move randomly and unpredictably. Fundamental analysis is a waste of time since no one can forecast stock prices.

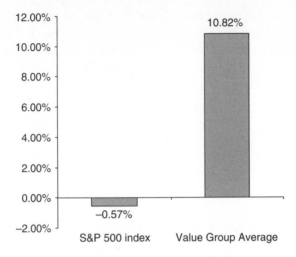

FIGURE 2.1   The 5-Year Average Return through 2003 of Ten "True Blue" Value Funds.

2003 for the 10 funds combined was 10.82 percent, or more than 11 percent higher per year than the S&P 500 index. The results can be seen in Figure 2.1.

What is so striking about Lowenstein's study is how little coverage it received in the financial media. I can't recall seeing anything about it until I stumbled upon it while doing a search on Google. The fact that a group of investors sharing the common philosophy of value investing avoided the flavor of the day (those stocks recommended in the *Fortune* article) and beat the market by a wide margin over a five-year period should have made headline news.

These "true blue" funds beat the market consistently over time, and that makes the point about value investing. But does this mean you can beat the S&P only by buying shares in one of these successful mutual funds? Not necessarily. I believe that a knowledgeable individual investor, without all the resources of big mutual funds, can beat the market on your own, without having to give up control of how their money is managed. How could that be possible? It's because the individual investor is not shackled by all the constraints that professional money managers have to deal with. In the investing world, the underdog has the edge.

In the Bible, Samuel I, Chapter 17, records one of the biggest upsets in military history. Today, the mere mention of the two participants, David and Goliath, evokes an image of the underdog beating the favorite. The story takes place in biblical Israel. The Israelites, led by King Saul, are fighting a battle with their Philistine oppressors when both sides face off on adjacent hills. The Philistines' most outstanding soldier is Goliath, who stands close to 9 feet tall in heavy armor that weighs 130 pounds by today's standards. He taunts the Israelites to send a soldier to fight him, but no one steps forward.

David, whose older brothers are serving among the Israelite troops, is sent by his father to bring them food. It is there that he sees Goliath's challenge firsthand and offers to fight him. Instead of wearing heavy armor, David faces Goliath with nothing more than a stick, a slingshot, and a few smooth stones. Goliath is furious and says: "Am I a dog that you come against me with sticks?" As Goliath approaches, David slings one of his stones, which hits Goliath's skull. Goliath falls to the ground, and David takes Goliath's sword and cuts his head off.

In the investing world today, institutional investors are the Goliaths. They are staffed by very bright people with unlimited resources and extensive teams of assistants. The largest 300 managers hold $7.5 trillion worth of stocks, 56 percent of the U.S. stock market's total capitalization of $13.2 trillion.[6] Does a knowledgeable investor, the modern day David, armed with nothing more than annual reports, 10-K filings and perhaps a copy of the Value Line Investment Survey, stand a chance to outperform these giants? Absolutely; in fact, most of the institutional investors' strengths are actually their weaknesses, and the knowledgeable investor has the advantage. My definition of a knowledgeable investor is one who purchases shares in a business (stock) for less than its underlying value. This type of investor is trying to get the most value for their dollar.

Evolution

Institutional investing has evolved over the past 30 years in ways that have handicapped their performance. In most years, more than 90 percent of institutional investors underperform the yardstick of stock performance, the S&P 500 index. After studying this phenomenon over the past several years, I have identified three stumbling blocks that make mediocre performance the norm for institutional investors:

1. Short-term time horizon.
2. Market cap limitations.
3. Restrictions on sector/geography/cash levels.

Short-Term Time Horizon

The money management business is a great business. If you gather assets and have adequate performance, investors will stay with you for a long time. Money managers usually charge a management fee of one percent of the total assets under management. If a firm has assets of $1 billion, the annual fee would be $10 million. There are more managers than you can shake a stick at with assets in the tens of billions of dollars, so a firm with $10 billion under management would generate management fees of $100 million per year! The goal for many firms is to retain what they have and gather more assets. If a firm slips up and has negative performance, there is a real fear of losing assets to another firm that is performing better.

The nature of the business has created an environment where institutional investors have to focus on short-term relative performance. The penalty for short-term underperformance would be an exodus of assets, resulting in lower management fees and early retirement for the portfolio manager. The distraction of how they have been performing over the past week, month, and quarter in relation to their peers causes money managers to go into self-preservation mode. In other words, they start thinking: "If I underperform and lose my job, how will I pay my country club dues and private school for my kids?"

Thus begins the slippery slope to mediocre performance. Instead of investing in what looks attractive on a valuation basis and holding for the long term, they begin buying what other managers are buying so as not to fall behind their peers in performance. A long-term view would prove disastrous to the financial health of the firm and their own job security. The measuring stick is not an absolute return but a relative return. For example, if fund A is down 20 percent and fund B is down 18 percent, the manager of fund B is having a happy day. It reminds me of the old joke of two hikers who see an angry bear approaching, so one of the hikers starts putting on a pair of running shoes. The other one says, "You can't outrun a bear!" So the first hiker answers, "I don't have to outrun the bear—I only have to outrun *you*." Absolute performance or outperforming the S&P 500 doesn't really matter. The goal now is to outperform the other funds in their category and a herd mentality sets in.

> *"An irresistible footnote: in 1971, pension fund managers invested a record 122% of net funds available in equities—at full prices they couldn't buy enough of them. In 1974, after the bottom had fallen out, they committed a then record low of 21% to stocks."*[7]
> —*Warren Buffett*

Market Cap Limitations

A recent survey of U.S. hedge funds shows that 241 firms, each managing more than $1 billion, held a combined total of nearly $1.2 trillion as of January 1, 2007.[8] There are also many mutual funds with at least $10 billion in assets, and in the investing game size does matter. Due to their size, institutional investors are in a catch-22 situation. The more money under management, the more fees they will generate. However, the size of their assets limits their selection of stocks to invest in and thus their ability to outperform the S&P 500 index. A firm with $1 billion in assets under management could not consider an investment in a company that has a $200 million market cap. If they bought 5 percent of the stock, or $10 million, it would hardly have any impact on the performance of the fund. That holding, no matter how well it did, would not be enough to move the performance needle.

Because of that, a mutual fund with $1 billion in assets has a very limited pond in which to fish. In order for a mutual fund to get adequate diversification (which is mandated by law), yet not wanting to own more than 5 percent of any one company (which triggers a whole bunch of SEC filings), the mutual fund would be able to invest in only about 800 companies that have a market cap of greater than $1 billion. There are close to 8,000 stocks traded on all the U.S. exchanges, yet portfolio managers with sizeable assets need to exclude close to 90 percent of them from their universe.

Restrictions on Sector/Geography/Cash Levels

Most institutional investors place an added burden on their managers by further restricting their investment universe. A sector fund can invest in only the sector or category that is identified in the fund's prospectus. If the fund happens to be a bank sector fund, the manager cannot invest in a retail company. The same goes for geography (certain countries or regions) that falls outside the fund's stated objective. If a great company, outside the fund's sector or geographical location, is trading at an extremely attractive price, the portfolio manager's hands are tied. Mr. Market could be giving away dollar bills for dimes, yet these managers would not be permitted to buy them.

> **Mr. Market**
> a metaphor created by Benjamin Graham to demonstrate the erratic price swings of the stock market. Based on Mr. Market's "moods" he can be euphoric (bid prices higher) one day and be depressed (drive prices lower) the next.

> *"Ben's Mr. Market allegory may seem out-of-date in today's investment world, in which most professionals and academicians talk of efficient markets, dynamic hedging and betas. Their interest in such matters is understandable, since techniques shrouded in mystery clearly have value to the purveyor of investment advice. After all, what witch doctor has ever achieved fame and fortune by simply advising 'Take two aspirins'?"[9]*
> *—Warren Buffett*

Many stock funds are also prohibited from holding cash and are mandated to be fully invested at all times. If prices of companies within the portfolio manager's universe are trading at sky-high valuations, the portfolio manager has no choice but to continue to plow their excess cash at even higher valuations. That was one of the reasons that technology funds back in 1999 continued to purchase shares of technology companies at nosebleed valuations. Quite simply, they couldn't hold cash in their portfolio. In this world, cash is a dirty four-letter word.

Your Edge

Knowing what you are up against, do you now see how you, David, has a big advantage? As a knowledgeable individual investor, you have none of these restrictions imposed on your selection of stocks. You know that over the short term, stock prices move based on fads and popularity, but over the long term (five years–10 years), stock prices move based on the earnings of the company. How could one not take the long-term view? To you, it should really make no difference if the latest government report came in a tenth of a percent higher or lower than expected, causing the stock market to take a dive. Over the long term, it doesn't mean a pile of beans. You use those opportunities to scoop up shares of great companies selling at fire-sale prices.

When the stock market reopened on September 17, 2001, the first trading day after the 9/11 terrorist attack, stock prices tumbled. The United States had just suffered the worst terrorist attack in history and investors panicked by selling. Multibillion dollar companies lost a big chunk of their market cap in one day. Tragic as the 9/11 attack was, does it make sense that a medical appliance and equipment maker, a car manufacturer, a money center bank, a semiconductor manufacturer, and a brokerage firm, should lose value if nothing fundamentally changed in their business? There will always be some type of crisis that causes people, especially Goliaths to react in irrational ways. It is during those times that you need to act and be ready to purchase companies on your target list. See Table 2.1.

> *Investment managers frantically trade long-term securities on a very short-term basis . . . hundreds of billions of dollars are invested in virtual or complete ignorance of underlying business fundamentals, often using indexing strategies designed to avoid significant underperformance at the cost of assured mediocrity.*[10]
> —*Seth Klarman, The Baupost Group*

TABLE 2.1   Institutions Panicked after 9/11, Putting Companies on Sale

Company	9/10/2001 Stock Price	9/17/2001 Stock Price	Return	Industry
Zimmer Holdings	$ 26.44	$ 25.25	−5%	Medical App. & Equip.
Citibank	$ 33.38	$ 31.14	−7%	Money Center Bank
Goldman Sachs	$ 72.62	$ 66.14	−9%	National Brokerage
Intel	$ 24.72	$ 22.37	−10%	Semiconductor
Ford	$ 16.21	$ 13.83	−15%	Auto Manufacturer
S&P 500 index	1,092.54	1,038.77	−5%	INDEX

You should back the truck up and purchase "ugly ducklings"—stocks that are not popular or are in boring industries. Since you don't have a whole bunch of restrictions imposed on you or need to worry about losing your job to a manager who shows slightly better performance than you over the past month, who cares what happens over the short term? The real success comes from investing in great companies that are selling at attractive prices and holding them for the long term.

The knowledgeable investor is not saddled with a small universe of stocks. Thousands of companies that offer great value in excellent industries but have small market caps are available to you as well. In addition to no limitations on market caps, there are also no restrictions to any particular sector or geographic location. It's like standing in line at a buffet in a Las Vegas hotel; you can choose to eat from any dish offered. Being an institutional investor is like being in that same buffet line but having high blood pressure, heart disease, and diabetes—their choices are severely limited and bland.

Cash is also not a bad thing to have in your portfolio. When the stock market bids up stock prices that are so disconnected from the underlying value of the company, cash is the place you want to be. It is better to earn whatever percent a money market is paying than to lose money. As long as you think of yourself as a knowledgeable investor and stay the course, you most definitely have the edge.

It is painful having money in the bank earning about 2%. Our investment philosophy is bimodal; either we invest in high returning opportunities or have the money in the bank or under our mattresses.
—Leucadia National Corporation,
Letter from the Chairman and President, 2005

EMT got it wrong when it said that markets are efficient *all the time*. I suggest that most value investors view markets as efficient about 85 percent to 90 percent of the time. It is the periods of time when irrational behavior takes over when markets become very inefficient and large profits can be made. As an individual investor, you're not constrained by the shackles that institutions wear. You do not have to focus on the short term, but can choose from companies regardless of market cap. You're not restricted on selecting companies based on their sector, where they are located, or how much cash you can hold in your portfolio. In fact, you have an enormous edge over institutional money. In the next chapter I share three lessons that when followed will allow you to take advantage of irrational behavior and profit from it rather than being part of it.

Key Points

1. The popular efficient market theory (EMT) is simply, provably wrong. History has shown that markets, at times, are extremely inefficient, especially when it comes to the prices of businesses.

2. The smart money does *not* follow the crowd, but instead seeks out exceptional stocks selling at bargain prices.

3. The 300 largest institutional investors control more than half of the stock markets' capitalization. But most underperform the market. This single fact shows how individuals using the principles of value investing can, indeed, beat the big mutual funds.

Chapter 3

Market Caveats:
Lessons from the Past

April 14, 2000 was an important milestone in the stock market as far as I am concerned. I can still remember the scent of spring as I made my way to the office that morning. An economic report was released before the market opened, and it caused Mr. Market to go into shock. Stock index futures immediately went *limit down*, which is the maximum price movement the stock index futures could fall in a given time span. Stock index futures could not begin trading until a "cooling off" period had passed or buyers appeared. The day went from terrible to downright ugly. The NASDAQ lost more than 9 percent and the S&P 500 index fell close to 6 percent. This capped off a week that plunged the NASDAQ 25 percent lower and the S&P 500 ended down more than 10 percent.

Only a few weeks earlier on March 10, the NASDAQ had hit an all-time high of 5,132. When the market closed on April 14, the NASDAQ stood at 3,321 for a loss of 35 percent in only 26 days. Looking at this drop in dollar terms is staggering—$2.3 trillion went up in smoke. In a very short timespan investors went from falling in love with Internet companies at extreme valuations to dumping them at any price. On March 27, eBay, Yahoo, and Amazon made all-time highs as investors bid up prices. Yet by April 14, eBay, Yahoo!, and Amazon had fallen an average of 42 percent from their peak. See Table 3.1.

After running in place over the next several weeks, the stock market continued to fall into the worst bear market since the Great Depression. Many market pundits over the coming weeks threw in their two cents as to what

TABLE 3.1 Declines from All-Time-Highs in Only 26 Days			
Stock	High 27-Mar-00	Close 14-Apr-00	18-day Loss
eBay	$255	$139	−45%
Yahoo	$205	$116	−43%
Amazon	$75	$47	−37%
Avg. percent decline from peak			−42%

caused the steep drop in prices. The most accurate cause was that valuations of stocks became "excessive." While not much changed in the fundamentals of these companies, most investors shunned stocks and would not buy them at any price. What caused such a quick shift in investor sentiment in such a short span of time? What lessons can we learn from successful value investors and how could one have avoided this meltdown?

Three Things to Keep in Mind

Looking back with the clarity of time, I see three lessons that investors should have learned about the stock market beginning with the events of April 2000. These lessons are not new; Ben Graham wrote about them in 1934 in his book coauthored with David Dodd, *Security Analysis*.

During the bull market of the late 1990s many on Wall Street forgot the rules, or said that they were outdated and no longer applied because we were in a "new paradigm." Once again, Wall Street showed investors that "there is nothing new under the sun." Don't overlook these three very important lessons that the stock market taught investors over the past several years.

Lesson 1: It's not a blip!

"Buy ABC Inc., the stock should double by the end of the week!" a good friend of mine told me at the height of the dot.com mania. I asked him what business the company was in. Looking at me as if I were from Mars, he said, "How should I know?" I then followed up with a few more stupid questions such as, "Does the company make money? How long have they been in business? Who is the CEO?" Needless to say, my friend swore off ever giving me moneymaking advice again.

This incident is not so strange or exceptional; it's typical. Many buyers of stocks forget that what they are buying is an ownership interest in an actual business, which has an underlying value. That underlying value of the business does not depend on the share price of the stock. Investors forget that stocks are not blips on a screen or numbers on a ticker. It is all too easy to make this mistake, instead assigning a dollar value to the business based on the price the stock is trading for. Simply because the share price of a stock climbs from $50 to $100, doesn't mean that the company is doing well. Investors confuse a rising stock price with a healthy and vibrant business. They judge the financial strength of a company on whether the stock price is rising or falling.

From December 31, 1999, to the day NASDAQ made its all-time high on March 10, 2000, Johnson & Johnson, a maker of health care products, saw its stock price fall by 23 percent. Many investors concluded that since the stock price was falling, so were the fortunes of the company. They couldn't have been more wrong. In fact, Johnson & Johnson's earnings were 11 percent higher in 1999 than they had been the year before and they also produced close to $4 billion of free cash flow (cash above and beyond what was needed to run their business). Hardly what one would call a struggling business!

Investors forget that the real driver of stock prices over time is the earnings of the company. Yet back in the mania, the thought of earnings was so—old-fashioned. In 1999, Juno Online Services announced an amazing business plan: They would offer free e-mail and Internet access, and they would spend a fortune on advertising over the next several years. How they would turn a profit was not disclosed. For this fantastic insight, the stock soared from $16 to $66 in only two days! Over the next several years the stock sank down into single digits.

There was a time when investors bought stocks, took pride in their ownership, and passed them on to their heirs. In 1973 the typical shareholder held a stock for five years. The average shareholder holds a stock today for less than 11 months. By forgetting that stocks are actually pieces of a real business, intelligent people turned the stock market into a casino by buying what was rising and selling what was falling, instead of buying undervalued assets.

Lesson 2: Mr. Market is Mental!

Ben Graham said that Mr. Market is bipolar and is not a very good appraiser of businesses. When stocks rise, Mr. Market gladly pays more than their value, and when stocks fall, he will unload stocks for much less than their worth.

During the stock market mania of 2000, Mr. Market was as bipolar as could be. For example, on March 17, 2000, Mr. Market valued a miniscule business, Inktomi, which was losing boatloads of money, at $25 billion. By September 2002, Mr. Market was depressed and revalued Inktomi at less than $40 million, or about 1/600th of its 2000 price. What was the real value of Inktomi? By the end of the year, Yahoo! bought Inktomi for $280 million.

When Graham was asked what holds most investors back from achieving success in the stock market, he said, "The primary cause of failure is that they pay too much attention to what the stock market is doing currently."[1] The real secret to investing was put best by Warren Buffett: "Be greedy when others are fearful and fearful when others are greedy." Not following the crowd is many times the wisest way to go.

I want you to keep this thought at the forefront of your mind: The stock market is there to serve you when you want it to serve you. Don't let bipolar Mr. Market influence your buy and sell decisions. You should be a buyer when, after careful evaluation, you can buy something for less than its intrinsic value. This simple logic could have saved investors billions of dollars.

Lesson 3: Price Is the Biggest Factor

I am sure that one day in the not so distant future, someone will ask, "What caused the worst market crash since the Great Depression that wiped out more than $7.4 trillion between March 2000 and October 2002?" The sad truth is that many investors stopped thinking for themselves. They let other people's judgments determine their actions. Ben Graham warned, "The really dreadful losses . . . were realized in those common-stock issues where the buyer forgot to ask, 'How much?'"[2] See Figure 3.1.

Stock prices became disconnected from the actual value of the company. *Barron's* cover story on December 27, 1999, was entitled "What's Wrong, Warren?" At the time of the article, Berkshire Hathaway Class A stock was down 23 percent while the S&P 500 was up 18 percent. Yet Berkshire's market cap was $83 billion and revenue was $2 billion. Yahoo's market cap was $120 billion—$37 billion greater than Berkshire's and it barely had $200 million in revenue. Investors bid up Yahoo!'s share price to the sky and pummeled Berkshire's stock. Neither valuation was in sync with reality.

A great company can be a lousy investment if you pay too much for its stock. The December 31, 1999, closing price of General Electric was $44 and Home Depot's was $65 (adjusted for splits and dividends). Over the next seven years investors who bought either of those two companies continued to see that company's earnings increase, yet the returns on their stock investments were under water. General Electric share price on December 31, 2006, was $37 and Home Depot's was $40. Buying a great company is no guarantee of high returns; you need to pay the right price, too.

Whenever I research a company, I try to figure out what the company does, how it makes money, and why I like it. I realize that a stock represents plants, employees, products or services, production, competition, and management. After looking at the financials of a company, you should ask yourself, "Do I want

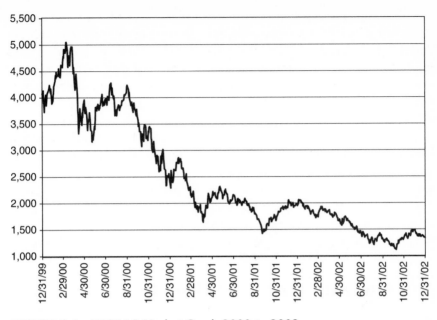

FIGURE 3.1   NASDAQ Market Crash 2000 to 2002.

to be in that business?" If the answer is no, move on. If you can't understand the business, put it in the "too hard" pile.

> *There are all kinds of businesses that Charlie [Munger] and I don't understand, but that doesn't cause us to stay up at night. It just means we go on to the next one, and that's what the individual investor should do.*[3]
> —*Warren Buffett*

Great value investors do not keep track of the stock price on a day-to-day basis. Some look at the stock price only a few times a year. If you think you have to constantly monitor price, you shouldn't be investing in stocks. The stock price will bounce around over the short term, but it will be the earnings of the company that propels the stock higher over time. Imagine if you owned a retail store and the weather forecast called for rain for the next few days. Since you would have fewer people in your store, sales would be down. Now imagine someone coming to you and valuing your business at 10 percent to 20 percent lower based on a few days of rain.

As absurd as that sounds, that is what Mr. Market does most of the time. I do my best to avoid the daily distractions of the stock market. The buy decisions I make are not based on what the stock price will do tomorrow or next week, but on how the company will continue to grow earnings over the next five years. There isn't a ticker on the front of homes registering a buy and sell price on a day-to-day basis, yet most homeowners get along just fine and have a very good idea what their home is worth.

Since I do not focus on the gyrations of Mr. Market, I can focus on what really counts: what price I would want to pay that will give me the biggest margin of safety and the highest return. A great company at a lousy price will not increase the size of your portfolio. As Warren Buffett quoting his teacher Benjamin Graham said, "Over the short term the stock market is a voting machine, (prices rise based on popularity), but over time the stock market is a weighing machine (stock prices will eventually go up, based on their earnings)."[4]

The Richest Man in the World

In 1988 the Los Angeles Lakers basketball team was on a roll. They had won back-to-back NBA championships, and it looked like they would win three championships in a row. That would be the best record since the Boston Celtics won an astonishing eight in a row from 1959 to 1966. Coach Pat Riley came up with the term "three-peat," which means winning three championships consecutively. The amazing part is that Riley trademarked the word. That meant that if a manufacturer put the word "three-peat" on a hat, shirt, or jacket, they had to pay Riley a licensing fee.

I wish I could have trademarked another quote heard by investors and their advisors almost daily. To many it seems sacrilegious to violate its holy message. The quote, which I'm sure you're familiar with, is "Don't put all your eggs in one basket." Yet I would contend that this quote explains what is responsible for more mediocre performance among investment portfolios than anything else I can think of. I would like to share with you how great investors diversify and manage their portfolios. By following the way the world's most successful investors manage their portfolios, you will give yourself a big advantage in the pursuit of higher performance.

At the beginning of the twentieth century, Andrew Carnegie was the richest man in the world. His life was literally a rags-to-riches story. Carnegie had come to the United States at the age of thirteen and worked as a bobbin boy in a cotton mill. After a series of jobs with railroad companies, he started his own business in 1865, which eventually grew into the Carnegie Steel Company, which, in turn, launched the steel industry in Pittsburgh. At age sixty-five, he sold the company to J.P. Morgan for $480 million (approximately $120 billion in 2007 dollars).

Carnegie had a much different take on the "don't put all your eggs in one basket" philosophy of investing. In fact, he said the exact opposite: "Concentrate; put all your eggs in one basket, and watch that basket."[6] I am sure that philosophy helped Carnegie become the richest man in the world. I would like to share with you the diversification strategy of some of the great stock investors of all time and explain how Carnegie's philosophy helped those investors accumulate millions and, in some cases, billions of dollars.

Understanding Your Investments

Several decades after Carnegie had received his huge buyout from J.P. Morgan at the formation of U.S. Steel, another great investor continued to expand on Carnegie's philosophy. British economist John Maynard Keynes wrote:

> As time goes on, I become more convinced that the right method of investing is to put fairly large sums into enterprises which one thinks one knows something about and in management of which one thoroughly believes. It is a mistake to think that one limits one's risk by spreading too much between enterprises about which one knows little.[7]

Profile: Andrew Carnegie

The original "self-made man," Carnegie was poor in his youth but amassed his fortune through a series of smart investments. He may even be thought of as the first value investor in the United States.

In 1864, Carnegie invested $40,000 in the Storey Farm in Pennsylvania and in one year he had earned more than $1 million in dividends and through sale of the property. By 1889 he had amassed a considerable fortune; that year he published an article called "Wealth,"[5] in which he explained his philosophy: Life should comprise two parts. First is the accumulation of wealth and second is distribution of wealth to worthy causes. The Carnegie Steel Company is his best-known corporation, which with merged assets controlled by another industrialist, J.P. Morgan, formed U.S. Steel in 1901. That was the first corporation in the United States with capitalization more than $1 billion.

From 1901 until his death in 1919, Carnegie followed his own philosophy and gave most of his wealth to charity. He funded libraries in most U.S. states and many other countries and gave away more than $350 million. His philosophy on distributing wealth was later embraced by Warren Buffett who is giving most of his assets back to society.

Keynes was probably the first *concentrated investor.* This is a type of investor who emphasizes the importance of understanding a business before making a purchase, and then invests a substantial portion of their capital in it.

Most people today diversify their investments among a broad range of investments and market sectors, without taking the time to research and understand what they are investing in. It seems so logical as an alternative to study the business model before putting money into a stock, but few practice this level of attention and research. Unfortunately, investors are likely to put more research into buying a car than they do in investing in a company. The problem of inadequate research is not limited to individual investors but professionals, too. Professionals who manage stock mutual funds usually have upwards of 100 different companies in their portfolios. How good can their seventy-eighth idea be? How well can they know all the companies in their portfolios? Warren Buffett once said: "If you have a harem of 40 women, you never get to know any of them very well."[8]

Professional investors who have fewer than 40 different companies are the exception rather than the rule and most professionals have portfolios that are doing the opposite of what Keynes suggested. I often wonder what type of return the bottom 10 percent of stocks in a portfolio with more than 100 stocks achieve. I would venture to guess they hardly add any value and probably take some away.

In 1929 Phil Fisher put out a shingle, began his investment counseling business, and soon after became a legend. He, too, invested in only a few companies that he knew very well. In his now classic book on investing, *Common Stocks and Uncommon Profits,* Fisher wrote:

> It never seems to occur to [investors], much less their advisors, that buying a company without having sufficient knowledge of it may be even more dangerous than having inadequate diversification.[9]

Fisher invested as much as 75 percent of his portfolio in his top three or four selections and held those companies for decades, the exact opposite of what most professional and novice investors do.

> *Diversification is only a surrogate, and usually a damn poor surrogate for knowledge, control and price consciousness.*[10]
> —*Martin Whitman, Third Avenue Management*

Fidelity fund star Peter Lynch called diversifying your portfolio among a broad range of businesses you don't understand, "diworsification." What usually ends up happening is that as soon as the stock price starts to fall, most investors panic and sell at a loss. Since they did not do much research into the company and don't understand the business, they let the stock market tell them the value of the company. The more they try to diversify, the worse the performance becomes; they never get to know much about any one company. Investing in only quality companies after understanding their businesses, gives you the highest probability for success.

The Dynamic Duo

Great investors like Warren Buffett and Charlie Munger continue to follow the ways of Keynes and Fisher by concentrating their portfolios with only their best ideas. After extensive research, Buffett would not hesitate to invest a large portion of his net worth in one stock. In fact, in 1963 Buffett invested close to 40 percent of his partnership's assets in American Express after judging how undervalued the share price was relative to the underlying worth. Buffett wrote:

> If you are a know-something investor, able to understand business economics and to find five to ten sensibly priced companies that possess important long-term competitive advantages, conventional diversification makes no sense for you.[11]

The same theme comes up again and again: Know what you are investing in and focus your investments among your best ideas. Diversification works against you when it is excessive. If you do your homework, you discover that there aren't that many good investments available at one time. The game would be a lot easier if there were always 30 to 40 great companies selling at fair prices. You really couldn't miss investing in any one of them. But the reality is, at any given time there are only a handful of great companies selling at fair or bargain prices.

Buffett and Munger do their homework and wait for the market to offer them a price that is a big discount from the companies' underlying value. Once that happens, they go "all in" because the opportunity may not present itself for months or—many times—years later. What is the magic number of stocks that a value investor should buy? Each master has his or her own idea of what is optimal, but it is fair to say it is certainly fewer than 20. After doing extensive research and becoming, according to Buffett, a "know-something" investor, he stated:

> If you really know businesses, you probably shouldn't own more than six of them. Very few people have gotten rich on their seventh best idea. But a lot of people have gotten rich with their best idea.[12]

Charlie Munger narrowed the number of stocks to have in a portfolio down to three. Great investors like Keynes, Buffett, and Munger have achieved outstanding performance over the long term by looking at the same stocks that the best and brightest of Wall Street have to offer. They achieved outstanding returns simply because they focused on their best ideas and invested accordingly.

I want to give you a hypothetical situation and it will become obvious to you why you should concentrate your portfolio in quality businesses. Imagine you are given $1 million and are told that you can invest it in any company within a 20-mile radius of your home. You also have access to each company's past 10 years of financial statements. However, there was only one caveat: You have to stick with your decision for the next five years. What would you do?

Before we tackle what you would do, let's discuss what you probably *wouldn't* do. I highly doubt you would open up the Yellow Pages and invest equally in every company that is within 20 miles of your home. Without working too hard, it wouldn't be difficult to discern the great, good, and poor companies in the pack. By just using a little bit of brain power, you most likely would avoid the poor companies and invest only in the great ones. You also wouldn't make a selection from the companies with the biggest advertisements in your local paper. Harry's Tires & Rims might be the place to go when it's time to change your tires, but when you start looking at it as a five-year investment, you would probably think twice about making that investment.

If you are a rational person, you would approach this challenge in a logical manner. You would first come up with the components of what makes a great business. After you have listed the criteria for a great business, you would then "look under the hood" and read the financials to see how well the company performed and how much money it made. Trying to select a company for your investment by only looking at the numbers would not give you a good understanding of the business. If looking just at the financials would make someone a successful investor, then accountants would be the richest people on earth.

Average stock investors buy stock in the same manner they buy lottery tickets. The greater the payoff and the sexier the story, the more they salivate. How else can you make sense of intelligent people buying stocks of companies that have very little chance of ever making money in rapidly changing industries? One reason investors do such silly things when it comes to buying stocks, which they would never do when investing in a private business, has to do with the way they think. Thinking about stocks as pieces of businesses makes all the difference in the world. Benjamin Graham wrote: "Investing is most intelligent when it is most businesslike."[13]

If you approach investing like Graham suggested, in a businesslike manner, you would want to concentrate on businesses that are easy to understand and have a consistent and predictable operating history.

Easy to Understand

Of all the companies listed on the New York, American, and NASDAQ stock exchanges, there are many that are difficult to understand and even harder to explain. Peter Lynch advised that one should "never invest in any idea you can't illustrate with a crayon."[14] You should be able to understand how the business makes money and what products or services the company sells. I'm not saying that you need to become an expert and understand everything about the company. I realize that you are not running the business on a daily basis and that you can't compete with the knowledge a middle manager who works within the company has, but you should have a working knowledge of how the company makes and spends its money.

The important things to understand about the business are the factors that will affect sales, earnings, and cash flow; all of which are very knowable. If you don't understand these factors, it will often be too late before you realize that the company is on the way down. Great companies like Harley-Davidson, Wells Fargo, and Costco can all be summed up in just a few words. These companies do not have many "moving parts" (i.e., motorcycles, money center bank, and wholesale shopping clubs) and each sticks to its knitting. If you can't figure out what the company does after five minutes, move on. Warren Buffett had this to say when encountering a business that is too difficult to understand:

> Investors should remember that their scorecard is not computed using Olympic-diving methods: Degree-of-difficulty doesn't count. If you are right about a business whose value is largely dependent on a single key factor that is both easy to understand and enduring, the payoff is the same as if you had correctly analyzed an investment alternative characterized by many constantly shifting and complex variables.[15]

Consistent and Predictable Operating History

After doing research on a company, only make a purchase if you are highly confident that its earnings and sales will be as consistent and predictable over the next five years as it has been in the past five years. Certain industries have very consistent and predictable operating histories. One example of an industry to avoid is the airline industry, which has proven to be very inconsistent and unpredictable. The price of fuel and the threat of terrorism can put a big damper on earnings and sales for long periods of time. A consistent operating history is very important when you are trying to predict future growth rates. If the past operating history is erratic, how can you project the future? Finding those companies that have a consistent long-term operating history is not such a daunting task. Out of a universe of all stocks traded on the U.S. exchanges, less than 200 have long-term (10 years), consistent, and predictable operating histories (sales and earnings).

Sticking with companies that consistently increase sales and earnings greatly minimizes your risk of permanent capital loss on your investment.

> *Predictability is a key part of valuing a company, with value determined by the amount of cash an enterprise can generate over time. If you can't understand the business, you can't value it. If you can't value it, you shouldn't own it.*[16]
> —*Larry Coats, Jr., Co-manager of the Oak Value Fund*

Take the Challenge

Knowing what companies to avoid is just as important as knowing what companies to focus on. By sticking with companies that have understandable businesses, a consistent operating history, and an enduring competitive advantage, you put the laws of probability in your favor. Like Warren Buffett, the next time you are searching for investments, have three boxes on your desk marked IN, OUT, and TOO HARD. Put anything you can't easily figure out in the TOO HARD box. By knowing what you don't know and sticking to what you do know, you will already be way ahead of the crowd.

The lessons written down by Benjamin Graham and David Dodd more than 70 years ago still apply today. Keep in mind that when you are buying a stock, you are buying a piece of a company. Once you buy the stock, let the fundamentals of the business tell you how well they are doing, not the daily change in the stock market. Lastly, *the price you pay for the stock will make the biggest difference on the return you get.* Once you find a handful of great businesses selling at attractive prices, buy them so they make up a large percentage of your portfolio. Great investors concentrate their investments in just a few stocks; shouldn't you?

Now that you are looking at stocks (pieces of a company) a lot differently from when you first picked up this book, the next chapter tells you how to make sure the companies you look at seriously are *great* companies.

Key Points

1. Asking the basic questions is the key to finding real value. Do you understand the business? Who are its managers? Is the company's operating history consistent and predictable?

2. The market is completely irrational and overreacts to just about everything. Were the market a person, it would be diagnosed as bipolar. So "following" the market is a big mistake ... but a very common one.

3. Diversification works best on a small scale, best applied in the small realm of businesses you understand thoroughly. You don't need 30 to 40 different stocks; less than 10 is ideal and certainly no more than 20.

Chapter 4

Are Great Companies Great Investments?

Stick with the Champs

When you view stocks as what they really are, pieces of businesses, you open your mind up to a whole new way of looking at the stock market. When you take this minority view, the stock tables in your local newspaper are not just a jumble of numbers and symbols that change on a daily basis. Instead consider them a business listing given to you by a business broker. You can have your choice of being partners with any company of your liking.

However the selection is overwhelming. With such a vast amount of stocks traded on U.S exchanges, where would you begin to narrow down your selection? Most investors would start with finding companies offering huge growth in new and exciting industries. They would go about trying to find the next Google, Microsoft or eBay. Very few would start their search by looking at companies that are household names, have been in business for decades, and have consistently produced excellent growth in both earnings and revenues.

It's only logical that great companies should be the first place you focus on before making an investment. However that is not how it works. In fact, many investors shun these companies and avoid them at all costs. There are several reasons why but the three that I have heard the most are:

1. Great companies are too efficiently priced.
2. Looking for the 10 bagger.
3. The financials get no respect.

Great Companies Are Too Efficiently Priced

Investors avoid great companies because they assume that they trade very close to their underlying value. Since they are so widely followed by institutional investors, everything known about them is already factored into the stock price. For example Dell, the largest direct computer systems company, is covered by 26 analysts from firms such as Citigroup, Bear Stearns and Goldman, Sachs while Daktronics, a manufacturer of scoreboards and display, is covered by only five from such firms as Noble Financial Group and Needham & Company. Since Dell is so widely followed while Daktronics is not, one would think that there is a high probability that Dell will be efficiently priced while Daktronics might not be.

Looking for the 10 Bagger

Many investors do not view stocks as pieces of businesses but instead look at them as lottery tickets. They want to buy a young company in an exciting industry and hope to make 10 or more times their investment. They are also willing to pay high prices for companies that oftentimes have not made a nickel of profit. Great companies, due to their size, can't grow that fast. It's virtually impossible for Wal-Mart's market capitalization to increase 10 times (to $3 *trillion*!) over a three-year period. Investors would rather roll the dice and try to find companies like Hansen Natural, a beverage seller, which was selling at $1 in the beginning of 2003 and was trading at $29 per share only three years later than to invest in well-known companies whose stock price has temporarily stalled out.

The Financials Get No Respect

Companies that have been in business for decades must be doing something right but most of the time do not receive any respect. Investors bid up the amount they would pay for each dollar of earnings on companies that have produced very little profit and at the same time sell off companies that have been cash generators for decades. With all its problems over the past several years Coca-Cola, founded in 1886, generated $5.5 *billion* in free cash flow in 2006 but commanded only a price-earnings (P/E) ratio of 21. While Electronic Arts, a software game maker (founded in 1982), generated $473 million in free cash flow in 2006, it commanded a P/E of 87!

At the end of the day, investors come to the conclusion that great companies will not be able to achieve adequate returns. Instead of investing in "Babe Ruth, Michael Jordan or Tiger Woods" type companies they spend their time trying to find the next big sleeper stock that will put them on easy street, usually to no avail.

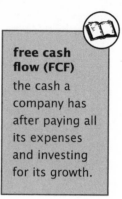

free cash flow (FCF) the cash a company has after paying all its expenses and investing for its growth.

Are Great Companies Great Investments?

Two economics professors wanted to see if investor prejudice is based on fact or fiction. Jeff Anderson and Gary Smith recently published a paper titled "A Great Company Can Be a Great Investment."[1] They took to task anecdotal evidence that often is presented as fact.

To identify a universe of great companies they studied the stock performance of companies identified by *Fortune* magazine as America's most admired companies, a listing *Fortune* has published since 1983. The 2005 list was based on a survey of 10,000 executives, directors, and securities analysts who first rated the companies in their industry on a scale of 1 to 10 in eight areas of leadership:

1. Innovation.
2. Financial soundness.
3. Use of corporate assets.
4. Long-term investment.
5. People management.
6. Quality of management.
7. Social responsibility.
8. Quality of products/services.

These votes were averaged to determine the rankings in each industry. The 10,000 participants were asked to name the companies they admire most in any industry from a list that included the two companies with the highest average scores in each industry and companies whose vote totals were among the top 25 percent the previous year.[2]

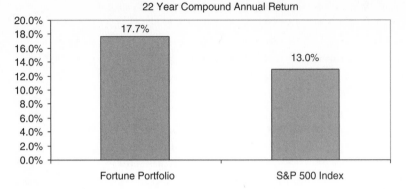

FIGURE 4.1   *Fortune's* Ten Most Admired Companies Portfolio.
Period: 1983–2005.

Anderson and Smith then invested an equal dollar amount in the 10 most admired companies, regardless of price and held them until the next survey. The following year, when the latest survey had been published, they simply sold their positions and bought the new companies ranked in the survey. To see if their results were robust, they used different start days to make sure that every investor could replicate the results even if they received *Fortune* several weeks after publication. One set of calculations used the first trading day as the date of publication (the magazine goes on sale several days before the publication date so an investor would have had ample time to buy the stocks in the survey). In other calculations they used the first trading day 5, 10, 15, and 20 trading days from the date of publication. The result was impressive and, to say the least, an eye opener. It didn't matter which starting date was used; every one of those calculations outperformed the S&P 500 index over the 22-year period (1983–2005). The *Fortune* portfolio produced an average annual return of 17.7 percent, outperforming the S&P 500 return of 13 percent. See Figure 4.1

I asked Professor Smith to run the calculations to determine how many years the *Fortune* portfolio had underperformed the S&P 500. In the real world, very few investors would stick with a strategy that would underperform the S&P 500 index for long periods of time. The results were even more amazing given how simple and elegant this approach was. Over the 22-year period, the *Fortune* portfolio beat the S&P 500 index 14 years and underperformed in only 8 years. This strategy had only two periods during 22 years when it underperformed the S&P 500 index for 2 consecutive years. That is a track record that most money managers would give their eye teeth to have. To put it into perspective, only one money manager, Bill Miller of Legg Mason, has been able to outperform the S&P 500 index every year for 15 years in a row.

The 2007 Ranking of *Fortune*'s Most Admired Companies

1. General Electric
2. Starbucks
3. Toyota Motor
4. Berkshire Hathaway
5. Southwest Airlines
6. FedEx
7. Apple
8. Google
9. Johnson & Johnson
10. Procter & Gamble

These companies are the giants in their industry; most have long records of producing consistent earnings and revenue, and increasing their competitive advantage within their industries. Although this group of "boring" big companies tends to get shunned because of the misconceptions I mentioned earlier, based on Anderson and Smith's research, buying them would have enabled an investor to do something that more than 90 percent of money managers are unable to do, and that is outperform the S&P 500 index.

Stick with the Champs

Anderson and Smith have done a great service to investors. By pointing them in the right direction and sticking with proven winners, they have shown the way to higher returns. The next time someone comes up to you with a stock tip about the next great company that is about to zoom, I suggest you smile and hold onto your wallet. Great companies do make great investments. By definition, great companies excel in the products or services they offer to their customers. Concentrating your attention and research in these companies, buying them at an attractive price and holding for the long term, will eventually increase your net worth.

Cigar Butts and Aircraft Carriers

My youngest son's birthday is in the first week of December. Despite all the presents he receives, there is only one present he actually plays with all year round—his toy Hess truck. For the past 40 years, Hess has introduced a new toy truck with real working parts. The coolest feature has to be the working lights. My son stays busy for long periods of time going under couches, beds, and chairs in the dark, pushing his truck around the house.

When I approached the counter to pay for the truck one December, I glanced at the magazine rack. Year-end editions of financial magazines were displayed for sale. Almost every end-of-year issue of financial magazines has a list of stocks that the reader should purchase. The lists range from 3 to 10 stocks that every investor must have in his or her portfolio. One year I counted all the stocks listed in *Fortune*, *Money*, and *Forbes* and I came up with more than 75 stocks! I know publishers are in the business of selling magazines, and at that time of year stock lists are crucial for sales. But what is most interesting to me is that very rarely is the same stock on the list for two years in a row. It seems to me that these lists are a revolving door of ideas with a shelf life of no more than one year. I am sure that great investors did not achieve their wealth by continually selling all their stocks in December and buying different ones in January.

Unfortunately, most investors do exactly that, each year selling off their old holdings to purchase new ones. Warren Buffett recommends that when investing act as if you were given a punch card and were allowed only 20 punches for your lifetime. Knowing you had only 20 punches, how would you look at each investment before you made it? I'm sure you would view each purchase from that moment on with much more scrutiny. No more taking flyers on a hot stock or building a Noah's Ark portfolio: a little bit of everything. By having this kind of attitude, you immediately gain an edge over other investors who make thousands of transactions and may take only a superficial look, at best, at each company.

Now that you have a punch card in hand that will be taken away from you after 20 holes are punched, where should you begin looking for ideas? While there are many types of businesses to choose from, I want to focus on two: "cigar butt" businesses and "aircraft carrier" businesses.

Buying a mediocre business at a low price and counting on some good fortune to cause the stock to rise, giving you a chance to make a decent return on your investment, was called the "cigar butt" approach to investing by Buffett. Why did he call these investments cigar butts?

A cigar butt found on the street that has only one puff left in it may not offer much of a smoke, but the "bargain purchase" will make that puff all profit.[3]

All the companies I would classify as cigar butts are trading at very cheap prices and have little to no debt. In most cases they are selling at cheap prices for valid reasons related to the declining fortune the company or industry is in. On a side note, Buffett put cigar butt investing first when he wrote his list of Mistakes of the First Twenty-Five Years.[4]

The main drawback for this approach is that after you get the "pop" and the stock goes up, you need to take your profit and move on. There is no continuity, and you always have to be looking for more cigar butts to buy.

TABLE 4.1　A Few of the Companies Owned by Berkshire Hathaway		
Company	Cost*	12/31/2006 Market Value
M&T Bank Corp.	$ 103	$ 820
The Washington Post	$ 11	$1,288
Moody's Corp.	$ 499	$3,315
Wells Fargo & Co.	$3,697	$7,758
American Express	$1,287	$9,198
Coca-Cola Co.	$1,299	$9,650

*Dollars expressed in millions
Source: Berkshire Hathaway Annual Report, 2006.

Charlie Munger, vice chairman of Berkshire Hathaway, had a profound impact on Buffett's thinking. Munger believed in paying a fair price for good businesses and influenced Buffett to focus on quality businesses because their best moneymaking days were ahead of them. Of course, when you find a quality business selling at a great price, you hit pay dirt, as Buffett did with the *Washington Post*, Coca-Cola, Moody's, and Wells Fargo, to name a few. See Table 4.1.

I, too, like to focus on quality businesses that have been around for a while. Companies with 10-plus years of operating history give you a sense of confidence that the business is a good one. Companies that are 50 years and older survived the cold war, the Vietnam War, Watergate, recessions, inflation . . . well, you get the idea. I call these companies aircraft carriers since they have weathered many a storm and continue to plow ahead. Only quality businesses are able to survive over long periods of time, and those are the ones I want to be partners with.

Coca-Cola went public in 1919; the stock sold for $40 per share. The Chandler family bought the whole business for $2,000 back in the late 1880s. So now it goes public in 1919, $40 per share. One year later it is selling for $19 per share. It has gone down 50% in one year. You might think it is some kind of disaster and you might think sugar prices increased and the bottlers were rebellious. And a whole bunch of things. You can always find reasons that weren't the ideal moment to buy it. Years later you would have seen the Great Depression, WW II and sugar rationing and thermonuclear weapons and the whole thing—there is always a reason. But in the end if you had bought one

> *share at $40 per share and reinvested the dividends, it would be worth $4 million now* (author's note: 2006 value–$5.6 million). *That factor so overrides anything else. If you are right about the business you will make a lot of money. The timing part of it is a very tricky thing so I don't worry about any given event if I got a wonderful business what it does next year or something of the sort.*
> —Warren Buffett speaking with MBA students—
> Florida State University, 1998

Quality Businesses

There are not many companies that are able to pass through my filters for quality. I was able to identify less than 100 companies that have market caps greater than $1 billion, 10-plus years of consistent operating history, high returns on equity, and little to no debt.

> *We have tried occasionally to buy toads at bargain prices with results that have been chronicled in past reports. Clearly our kisses fell flat. We have done well with a couple of princes—but they were princes when purchased. At least our kisses didn't turn them into toads. And, finally, we have occasionally been quite successful in purchasing fractional interests in easily-identifiable princes at toad-like prices.[5]*
> —Warren Buffett

While Wall Street likes to know a little about a lot of companies, you can focus on your own short list of companies and get to know a lot about them. There are many value investors who have achieved excellent long-term performance by focusing on a universe of less than 50 companies.

Load Up and Hold 'Em

Since there are so few quality companies, when they do become available at an attractive price you should load up on them. The world of investing attracts the smartest minds and, needless to say, is a very competitive place. Quality companies do not trade at attractive prices for very long.

In an investing lifetime, there are usually a handful of investment decisions that make up most of a person's net worth. For example, if you bought a four-bedroom apartment on New York's Park Avenue in the 1950s and a summer home on the ocean in the Hamptons in the 1960s, your net worth would be somewhere in the eight digits. If those two investments are the only ones you made in 50 years—you are having a happy retirement.

Selecting a good investment is not the difficult part; sticking with it is what is challenging for most people. When Buffett bought a large block of the *Washington Post* in 1973 to 1974, it was trading at a quarter of its underlying worth. It was a quality business run by very competent management when Buffett invested a large percentage of his assets in the stock—close to $11 million. Over 30 years later, that investment paid off handsomely for him, as the original $11 million was then worth more than $1.3 billion.

Another great advantage in holding on to substantial investments in quality companies for the long term is deferring capital gains taxes. The only time you pay tax on the appreciation of your investment is when you sell. Say, for example, you were lucky enough to have bought 1,000 shares of Berkshire Hathaway stock in 1965 at $25 a share, for a total investment of $25,000. If you had held them till 2006, those 1,000 shares would have grown to $105 million! Since Berkshire Hathaway does not pay any dividends, take a guess as to how much tax you would have had to pay over the past 42 years. Not one dime! You would be liable for taxes only when you sold the shares, but until then your money would continue to grow as the stock price rose.

What advantage do you get by investing for long stretches of time in quality companies? A very large one, based on the way U.S. income tax works. Let's say you invested in a quality business in 1976 and held it for 30 years. Also assume that over that period your investment grew at a rate of 15 percent per annum. It's only when you decided to sell in 2006 that your tax bill of 15 percent (long-term capital gains—the tax owed if you hold a stock one year and a day) was due. Your return after tax works out to 14.4 percent annually. See Figure 4.2.

On the other hand, if you made the same investment but had to pay a 15 percent tax bill at the end of each year, your return after 30 years would net you 12.75 percent. The difference of 1.65 percent over the long term is huge. The difference between a 14.4 percent return and a 12.75 return on a $10,000 initial investment over 30 years is more than $188,000. Taking advantage of the way income taxes work—by sitting on your hands and doing nothing—gives you a tremendous edge.

The real magic is so simple, logical, and rational that it always surprises me that more people don't do it. Make a substantial investment in a quality company at an attractive price and hold it for the long haul. The rest, as they say, is commentary. As Charlie Munger likes to say, "Investing is where you find a few great companies and then sit on your ass."[6]

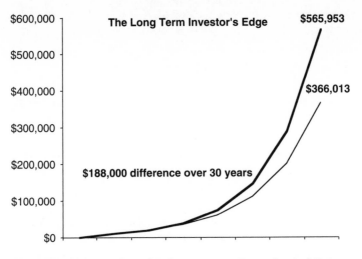

FIGURE 4.2 Benefits of Delaying Long-Term Capital Gains.

Key Points

1. If you think of investments as lottery tickets, you will also be willing to pay too much for stocks. There's a chance you'll profit, but it's a long shot.

2. You will always do better staying with proven winners, those boring but consistent companies. Fast-profit stock tips are exciting, but you will be better off rich and bored.

3. Take Buffett's advice: Invest like you have a punch card with only 20 punches. You will then invest in only your best ideas. Stick to quality companies and hold them for the long term. The big money is made by sitting not trading.

Who's in Charge? Management Counts

Getting Comfortable with Management

Good managements produce a good average market price, and bad managements produce bad market prices.[1]

—Benjamin Graham

When I look at management I ask myself, "Do I feel comfortable being their partner?" When I buy a share of stock, I'm not buying a wiggle on a chart. I view myself as an owner and I want to make sure management is focused on increasing shareholder value. If not, I'd be making a pretty lousy investment. I want to see if management's and shareholder's interests are aligned.

In the past this was much more difficult for the average investor to find out than it is today. Securities analysts used to travel extensively across the country meeting with management and having quarterly conference calls with them. Unless you worked for a major brokerage firm you had no chance of having a CEO of a multibillion company return your phone call. Institutional investors, who manage in many cases tens of billions of dollars, had a big advantage over the little guy as they were privy to company news ahead of the average investor.

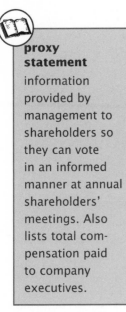

transparency
disclosure of a
company's finan-
cial reporting so
investors can get
a more accurate
understanding
of the financial
condition of the
company.

**proxy
statement**
information
provided by
management to
shareholders so
they can vote
in an informed
manner at annual
shareholders'
meetings. Also
lists total com-
pensation paid
to company
executives.

The Securities and Exchange Commission (SEC) did something about this glaring advantage that professionals had and implemented Regulation Fair Disclosure, or Reg FD in October 2000. It mandated that all publicly traded companies must disclose material information to all investors at the *same time*. The regulation sought to stamp out selective disclosure, in which some investors (often large institutional investors) received market moving information before others (often smaller, individual investors). Regulation FD changed fundamentally how companies communicate with investors, by bringing better *transparency* and more frequent and timely communications, perhaps more than any other regulation in the history of the SEC.[2]

At the end of 2006, the SEC implemented another ruling that required that executive compensation must be provided (in plain English) in the company's *proxy statement*. Companies are now required to provide investors with a clearer and more complete picture of their executives' total compensation. No longer are investors faced with the task of trying to piece together how much key personnel were paid in salary, stock options, benefits, and perks. The new rule also requires that much clearer information be disclosed regarding financial relationships between executives, directors, significant shareholders, and their immediate family members. You can now find out if the CEO's wife is being paid a consulting fee for designing the corporate office. There is also a web site that sifts through all the files and presents in a clear, easy to ready format all salaries, bonuses, and perks of executives of public companies.

Proxy Statement

The proxy statement gives the investor a wealth of information on how management is being compensated and what incentives are driving them. People respond to incentives and the proxy statement is telling me what type of incentives they are responding to. Is management's bonus based on earnings growth, the sale of the business, beating a certain average, or a host of other incentives that the compensation committee outlined? When reading the proxy report, we want to make sure that management and shareholder interests are on the same page.

Over the past decade, many companies awarded their top management through the granting of stock options. The conventional wisdom for rewarding stock options was that it aligned management's incentives with shareholder's interests. However, that didn't always turn out to be the case. If management's compensation was tied to the price of the stock and the stock price was tied to earnings, then the incentive for many top managers was to make sure earnings rose. Sometimes dishonest managers made sure earnings rose by cooking the books.

The SEC sued Xerox in 2002 for manipulating earnings during the late 1990s. Upper management used a whole bunch of tricks to show that the company was making more money than they actually were. During this period, the value of options exercised by the Xerox CEO was more than $20 million, almost three times the value of options exercised over the prior five years.[3] Xerox was not alone where pumping up earnings coincidentally happened with the exercise of options and sale of shares. Waste Management, Tyco, Enron, and Computer Associates are just some of the companies that engaged in this illegal practice. Instead of aligning upper management with shareholders, compensating them with stock options produced the opposite result: It encouraged management to manipulate earnings so that the stock price would rise.

In 2006 another scandal involving backdating options came to light. It seems that when companies granted options to their executives, it so happened that the grants occurred on days when the stock price was at its lowest. The probability of this happening on a consistent basis was calculated by the *Wall Street Journal* to be 1 in 6 billion. More than 2,000 companies and their executives are involved and it seems that management and shareholder interests were not aligned at those companies.

Heartland Express, Inc., is a good example of when management and shareholder interests are aligned. Heartland, a trucking company, was founded by Russell Gerdin in 1978 with 4 people in the office and 16 trucks.[4] In 2006 Heartland had $585 million in revenue, a strong balance sheet, and no debt. Investors have been handsomely rewarded: $1,000 invested when the company went public in November 1986 was worth more than $34,000 as of December 31, 2006.

How does Heartland compensate Mr. Gerdin, the founder and CEO? By looking at Heartland's 2006 proxy report[5] you can gain insight into the way management thinks about their company. The section titled Executive Compensation shows Mr. Gerdin's salary for the three years ending 2005 as $300,000—that's all he receives. He doesn't get any stock options or long-term incentives as part of his compensation, either. Since Mr. Gerdin owns about 35 percent of the company, he believes his compensation should come from the increased value of the company's stock.

> *At Mr. Gerdin's request, his salary has remained the same since 1986, and he has never been paid a bonus.* Mr. Gerdin receives an incentive through appreciation in the market value of the Company's stock. Because of Mr. Gerdin's request, the Compensation Committee did not consider or recommend an increase in annual compensation or any incentive compensation for Mr. Gerdin. Thus, corporate performance directly affects Mr. Gerdin, but not through his compensation by the Company.[6]

Another example of prudent compensation that is shareholder friendly can be found at Kinder Morgan Management, LLC. The company puts its shareholder money where its mouth is and specifically tells shareholders what their managers *do not receive:*

> Unlike many companies, we have no executive perquisites and, with respect to our United States-based executives, we have no supplemental executive retirement, non-qualified supplemental defined benefit/contribution, deferred compensation or split dollar life insurance programs. We have no executive company cars or executive car allowances nor do we offer or pay for financial planning services. Additionally, we do not own any corporate aircraft and we do not pay for executives to fly first class. We are currently below competitive levels for comparable companies in this area of our compensation package; however, we have no current plans to change our policy of not offering such executive benefits or perquisite programs.[7]

Other examples of CEOs that have large shareholdings in their company, take very modest salaries, and do not receive any stock options are Warren Buffett (Berkshire Hathaway), Ian Cummings and Joseph Steinberg (Lecuadia National Corporation), Weston Hicks (Allegheny Corporation), and Willard Oberton (Fastenal Company). By seeing how much or how little money is lavished on the CEO, you can get a very good impression of how management values the company's money.

Companies can't hide the way they compensate management. SEC regulations clearly state that material information must be disclosed in a public filing. When I read some of the public filings, I sometimes scratch my head and wonder how many ways management can obscure the way they lavish compensation on themselves. Here are just a few examples, which clearly demonstrate that management's and shareholder's interests are not aligned.

Phil Purcell, CEO—Morgan Stanley

Severance Package

During the spring of 2005, CEO Phil Purcell and his handpicked co-president Steve Crawford resigned from Morgan Stanley after causing a huge corporate turmoil. When Dean Witter and Morgan Stanley had merged several years back, Purcell had packed the board of directors with people loyal to him from his Dean Witter days. Morgan Stanley people had been pushed aside and had started leaving the firm. The company's financials and stock lagged behind those of its financial peers. Finally, after some large investors had been very vocal about wanting to give Purcell a pink slip, the board of directors gave in. However, since the board was packed with Purcell's cronies, they voted him an absurd severance deal. Purcell's exit package was estimated at $106 million, including a $44 million cash bonus and retirement package.

> *The salary of the chief executive of the large corporations is not a market award for achievement. It is frequently in the nature of a warm personal gesture by the individual to himself.*[8]
> —*J.K. Galbraith*

If that pay package weren't enough to make you wonder what they were thinking, co-president Steve Crawford's package surely is. Purcell had handpicked Crawford for his position as co-president only three and a half months before he resigned. For being on the job only about 100 days, Crawford received an exit package of $32 million! There were a few other perks thrown in for good measure. The company agreed to pay former CEO Purcell's secretary ($1.8 million), donate to his favorite charities ($2.9 million), and award other lifelong benefits ($3.1 million).[9]

Bill Butler, President—Aaron's Sales & Lease Ownership Division

Driving Lessons

Aaron Rents specializes in renting and selling office furniture and, in 2005, also sponsored a driver development program originated by professional race car driver Michael Waltip. They spent $890,000 in 2005 and nearly $1 million in 2006 on behalf of the company president's two sons and counted it as a market expense! It should raise some eyebrows that shareholders' funds were spent on a race car driving school for the president's two sons.[10]

Leonard Schaeffer, Former Chairman and CEO—WellPoint, Inc.

Office Space

When WellPoint acquired Anthem, Inc. a few years ago, a question arose as to how much compensation was to be paid to retiring WellPoint CEO Leonard Schaeffer. The proposed retirement package was somewhere between $37.5 million and $260 million. The lack of clarity should have been a big warning sign about lack of disclosure. Making matters worse, WellPoint then disclosed that they'd entered into a five-year lease with Schaeffer for office space at $186,507 per year plus a $6,000 annual parking fee. This was for space that had cost WellPoint $240,000.[11]

Shareholders should be outraged by these huge payouts and company expenses since in reality it was shareholder money that was being given away as part of a high-level buddy system. The new federal regulation requires that companies disclose material information, but there is nothing in the regulations that requires you to read them. You should look to invest in companies where shareholder's and management's interests are aligned. Not every manager of a publicly traded company acts like a kid left in charge of the candy store. There are some terrific managers who create cultures of frugality and have seen their bottom lines and stock prices soar.

Here are a few examples of managers who concentrate on cutting costs while at the same time growing their businesses. These managers have a high regard for shareholders and have been great creators of shareholder value.

Bob Kierlin, Former CEO and Co-Founder—Fastenal Company

The Cheapest CEO in America

A few years ago, *Inc.* Magazine listed Bob Kierlin, former CEO of Fastenal Company, a wholesaler and retailer of industrial supplies, as the "cheapest CEO in America."[12] Kierlin loves a bargain, clips coupons from the Sunday papers, and never pays retail. While CEO, he drove an Oldsmobile, kept his salary at $120,000 for decades, and did not have a secretary. Kierlin and his partner Stephen Slaggie, built Fastenal from a start-up in 1967 to a company that has more than 1,500 stores in the United States and overseas. Kierlin says, "Frugality is an attitude you develop. Once you have it, it sticks with you in everything in life." The corporate culture is one that reflects the founders' values. The employees realize that watching pennies will save dollars and grow their bottom line. Fastenal's net profit margin (five-year average) is 9.6 percent, more than twice the Miscellaneous Fabricated Products industry average of 4 percent.[13]

Alan C. "Ace" Greenberg, Former Chairman—The Bear Stearns Companies, Inc.

Counting Paper Clips

Alan C. "Ace" Greenberg, former chairman of Bear Stearns (NYSE:BSC), sent memos to his partners on the impact that saving paper clips would have on the company's bottom line. In his book, *Memos from the Chairman,* Greenberg wrote memos about saving paper clips and rubber bands, reusing interoffice envelopes, excessive use of FedEx, and turning off lights and machines when leaving for the night. The theme of controlling costs comes up in almost every memo. Saving money at Bear Stearns is no accident; they are the result of counting pennies and leaving behind a corporate culture that holds saving money in high regard.

Sam Walton, Founder—Wal-Mart Stores

Two to a Room

Sam Walton, founder of Wal-Mart Stores (NYSE:WMT), the largest corporation in the world with sales of more than $346 billion (2006), built his company on the value of frugality. Walton says, "There's no two ways about it: I'm cheap." One of his buyers recounts how, when on buying trips, he and colleagues slept two to a room; ate at family restaurants; and stayed at Holiday Inns, Ramada Inns, and Days Inns. Cabs were off-limits on these trips, and expenses could never exceed 1 percent of their purchases. Walton also made sure that buying trips were as short as possible and that his buyers put in a full workday each day of a trip.[14]

The corporate culture Walton promoted was "A dollar saved is a dollar passed on to the customer." For most other companies, a dollar saved is a dollar passed on to fill the pockets of management. Wal-Mart's competitive advantage of "Always low prices" is extremely hard to breach.

I'm sure the shareholders of Fastenal, Bear Stearns, and Wal-Mart are happy. Over the past 15 years, the stock prices of these companies have soared. When management fosters a culture of controlling costs, good things start to happen for the company. A good business will usually survive bad management. But when you own a piece of a good business with good management, your rewards will be higher share prices over the long term.

Thirty Minutes!

Not all case histories are as upbeat. If a CEO wanted to know how *not* to run their company's annual meeting, they should study the Home Depot annual stockholders' meeting held on May 25, 2006. It lasted only 30 minutes. CEO Bob Nardelli treated his shareholders not as owners or partners (which they happened to be), but as children who needed to be disciplined.

Right from the get-go, the meeting did not go well for shareholders. Nardelli was the only member of the board of directors in attendance; the other 10 directors perhaps had gotten lost on the way to the meeting and had just missed it. Shareholders who wanted to ask Mr. Nardelli questions were given a very limited amount of time. If a question or comment ran over the given time, the microphone was shut off. Nardelli also refused to answer most of their questions especially those pertaining to his compensation package.

Since he had taken over the CEO's chair at Home Depot in 2000 Nardelli's total compensation was $123.7 million, and he still had tons of stock options. While earnings did rise during his tenure, Home Depot lost market share to competitor Lowe's, stores were understaffed, and customer service was horrific. You would think that a guy who was making all that money would be just a bit humble, especially to his shareholders.

What a big contrast with Berkshire Hathaway's 2006 annual meeting. More than 24,000 shareholders traveled to Omaha, Nebraska, from all over the United States and the world, to be at the Woodstock of Capitalism. Berkshire's shareholders got to ask their chairman Warren E. Buffett (age 75) and vice chairman Charles Munger (age 82) any question they wanted for more than six hours. Every shareholder actually felt like an owner because that's the way their chairman treated them. If two senior citizens can sit for six hours and answer questions, certainly Mr. Nardelli (age 57) can.

For the sake of Home Depot ($90 billion market cap) and its shareholders, I hope that in the very near future Mr. Buffett will phone Mr. Nardelli and remind him who his real boss is. . . the shareholder. Then again, maybe not. Nardelli resigned his position in January 2007. His legacy: loss of market share, outdated stores, a lack of corporate focus, disgruntled shareholders, and a multimillion-dollar severance package.

What to Look for in a Manager

The goal of every management team is the same: to increase shareholder value. In a sense, you the shareholder are the absentee owner, and management is your working partner. When you invest your money in a company, you own a piece of that company. Since you can't be there every day to run things, you empower a board of directors to hire competent people to run your company.

What type of people do you want running your company? In addition to hiring managers who have the skills and talent needed to run the day-to-day operation, you also want them to be fair and honest. They should be managers who will allocate profits to increase shareholder value and not decrease it. They should also be open and honest when it comes to reporting the facts to shareholders. And you want them to have the courage and conviction to do what's best for the growth of the company and not simply copy the actions of other companies in their industry.

Measuring management is not an exact science and is most certainly not a black-and-white issue. There is a lot of gray that requires you to trust your instincts. Warren Buffett mentions three attributes that he looks for when sizing up managers:

1. Is management rational?
2. Are they candid with shareholders?
3. Do they resist the "institutional imperative"?

Is Management Rational? How Do They Allocate Capital?

The most important job management has is the allocation of capital. Allocation of capital to the bottom line, after all expenses and reinvestments into the business has been made, is the biggest factor determining shareholder value.

Let's assume you are the CEO of a profitable company. After doing the books, your chief financial officer sends you a memo and tells you some very good news. He informs you that the business had a terrific year and there is one small matter that you need to address: The company has $500 million in the bank. After paying all the company's bills, expenses, and reinvesting back into the business to keep it modern, the $500 million is called *free cash flow (FCF)*. What do you want to do with that money?

CEOs of successful businesses are faced with this challenge every year. Some businesses are "cash cows," generating such large amounts of FCF year after year

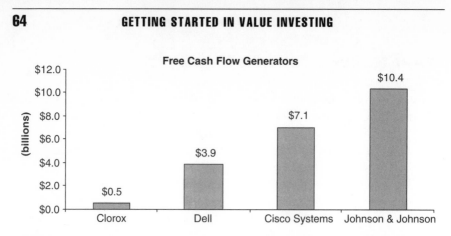

FIGURE 5.1 Companies that Generate Large Amounts of Free Cash Flow
Source: Morningstar 12-14-06 TTM.

that good and great CEOs are distinguished by how they allocate capital. See Figure 5.1.

In 2006, the CEO of Clorox had to invest $500 million of FCF while the CEO of Johnson & Johnson had to make a decision on $10.4 billion of FCF. It is at this point that managers need to act rationally in allocating capital because if they don't, they can very quickly destroy shareholder value instead of building it.

There are several ways they can go about allocating capital, keeping in mind they can also leave it in the bank earning about five percent. However, anybody can do that! Managers need to at least beat that rate and then some to add value to the company's worth by:

- Investing internally.
- Returning it to shareholders.
- Buying back shares.
- Making acquisitions.

Investing Internally If they invest the money back into the business and can generate a higher return than five percent that might be a good solution. However if the return on the investment will be less than five percent, Buffett would say that is acting irrationally.

Returning It to Shareholders Management may decide to return the money to shareholders, declaring and paying a dividend. Dividends are payments in cash or additional partial shares to shareholders. If the company already pays a dividend they may decide to increase it. There are several companies generating so much excess cash, that they increase the dividend each year. Then there are companies that have excellent management who have distinguished themselves

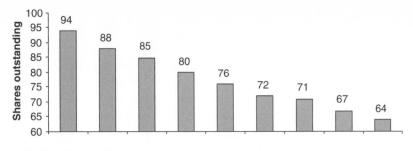

FIGURE 5.2 Timberland Shares Outstanding 1998–2006
Source: Value Line 12-13-06.

as very good allocators of capital that have never paid a dividend and have no intention to ever pay one. Shareholders get a much better return leaving cash in the hands of such skilled management.

Buying Back Shares If management believes that the share price of the company is undervalued compared to what they think the company is worth, they can elect to buy back their shares in the open market. If ABC Company's stock is trading for $35 a share and management believes it should be worth $70 a share, it would be an intelligent way to invest excess cash. This is beneficial to shareholders since it reduces the numbers of shares outstanding and increases the earnings per share.

Timberland Company, a manufacturer of footwear, has been a steady buyer of its shares for the past eight years. The company has repurchased more than 30 million shares on the open market since 1998. Since there are fewer shares outstanding in 2006 than there were in 1998, each shareholder retains a larger portion of the earnings. See Figure 5.2.

It also is a wise allocation by management since they are buying their own shares at an undervalued price. What you don't want to see is management that continually issues more shares which has the opposite effect—diluting the shares you own.

Making Acquisitions Companies make acquisitions of other companies and pay high prices for them, but at the end of the day these decisions do not always add to shareholder value. Instead of returning capital to shareholders, companies hoard cash to make a big acquisition that very rarely adds anything to the bottom line. Sometimes it seems that a CEO wakes up one morning and decides to acquire a company. By lunchtime he or she will have reports done by middle managers advising that the deal makes sense, and in fact that it's a stroke of genius. Projections and assumptions, however unrealistic, will be used to make it look good on paper. Buffett said that he has "never seen a proposed deal that didn't look good on paper."[15]

Keep a watchful eye on the cash that a company has and how they spend it. If management is disciplined and rational, they will do the right thing and create value. Simply because a company is generating excess cash flow doesn't mean they need to spend it on something foolish. There are very few managers who have the skill and discipline to acquire other companies. Most of the time managers pay too high a price for the acquired company and let their egos get the best of them. When you see companies constantly acquiring other companies it should set off an alarm bell. Why does management need to buy growth? Have they run out of ways to expand their business internally? History has shown that acquisitions don't always increase shareholder value. There are some managers who have done an excellent job of acquiring companies, but by and large most acquisitions do not add much to shareholder value.

> When a chief executive officer is encouraged by his advisers to make deals, he responds much as would a teenage boy who is encouraged by his father to have a normal sex life. It's not a push he needs.[16]
> —Warren Buffett

On January 10, 2000 America Online (AOL) acquired Time Warner for $182 billion. It was the largest merger in history and it combined the Internet's top service provider with the world's number one media conglomerate. The combined company was called an "unprecedented powerhouse" and a "merger of equals" by Wall Street analysts. The combined company, AOL Time Warner, was then worth $350 billion, but within a few short years more than $200 million of that market cap was gone. In 2002 AOL Time Warner reported a loss of $99 billion—the largest loss ever reported by a company. After dropping AOL from its name, Time Warner was valued at a dismal $85 billion. Instead of increasing shareholder value the management of both companies had found a way to destroy it.

Candid with Shareholders: Are They Sincere and Truthful?

Simply put, the CEO's annual report letter is written to you the shareholder, by the chief executive office or chairperson; to inform you of what happened in the past year. In addition, they will often state their goals for the company for the next year, pat themselves on the back for a job well done, or not often enough, point out their shortcomings. This also gives you insight as to where management's focus is and whether they treat shareholders like owners.

When reading the annual reports, I look for the number of times the CEO gives praise to others and uses self-effacing humor, which are the hallmarks of good leadership. Not taking yourself too seriously and lavishing praise on others, is usually the sign of a leader who feels secure in their position and brings out the best in others. Conversely, if the word "I" comes up with every great thing the company did over the past year, you should take that as a warning sign. Those are the signs of the CEO who wants to be the bride at every wedding and the corpse at every funeral—it's all about "me"!

Wal-Mart's 2006 shareholder letter was written by Rob Walton, chairman of the board and the founder's son. He stressed Sam Walton's fundamental principles of being a good and respectful employer, improving the customer shopping experience, being a responsible community citizen, and maintaining the highest level of integrity. The letter was less than one page and right to the point.

Willard D. Oberton, CEO and President of Fastenal began his 2005 letter to shareholders talking about the new initiatives the company had begun the previous year to help improve customer service, enhance career opportunities for employees, and increase returns for shareholders. Oberton went on for the next three pages with details about the company's success and shortcomings over the past year. His enthusiasm for the business came through loud and clear.

By reading the letters in the annual reports, I get insight into the person leading the company and what they value. Someone once told me to go into business only with someone you would feel comfortable giving your house keys to. After reading five years of shareholder letters, I ask myself that same question. I want to feel comfortable with the management running my company.

Resisting the "Institutional Imperative": Are They Lemmings or Leaders?

I remember when I was growing up and did something wrong, my father would sit me down, give me a stern look and demand an explanation. Often, my reply was, "But Dad, everyone else was doing it." Doing what everyone else is doing is still the excuse for companies acting like lemmings and jumping off the cliff. Follow the leader is not a game relegated to the playground; it is still played in boardrooms across the United States.

Between 1975 and 1982, U.S. commercial banks could not lend money quickly enough to financially and politically shaky Latin American governments. At one point the debt to Latin America was more than half of the region's market value of all goods and services (gross domestic product). Why did banks fall over themselves and continue to lend money to these countries? Because everyone else was doing it. Look for managers who stand apart and do not lead their companies down the road to disaster.

Why do intelligent managers make stupid mistakes? Warren Buffett has learned, through his many years of experience, that the "institutional imperative" takes over. Simply put, the institutional imperative is doing dumb things just for the sake of doing them.

The Annual Report

The next important document you should read is the company's annual report.

I happened to be driving with my two young sons through my old neighborhood one day and like my father before me, I bored them with details of my old stomping grounds. They got to see the schoolyard where I had played stickball and basketball and the house I had grown up in. As we headed home, I pointed out to them the library where I had spent a good deal of my time as a youngster and teenager. For the rest of the drive home my kids teased me about being a nerd and a geek.

My love of reading began when I was in first grade. My mother signed me up in a children's book of the month club. Around the first of each month, I eagerly ran home from school hoping the monthly selection would arrive in the mail. I remember ripping apart the cardboard envelope and reading the book cover to cover. I still get excited when I see the mailman hoping my book order from Amazon.com is there.

Reading has served me well in my vocation as manager partner of a limited partnership and as editor of a newsletter. I spend a large part of my day reading. For every company that is on my target list (about 75 companies), I read the past 5 years of annual reports as well as the annual reports of their competitors. I start with the oldest one first and then read them sequentially. I want to see if the promises made and goals set in one year were kept in the next.

For example, if Walgreens is on my target list, I read the oldest available annual report first. I then read the same year reports of Rite-Aid, CVS, and Long's Drug Stores, Walgreens' competitors. I need to see how each company dealt with the same industry conditions and ask myself why one company thrived and another slumped. This information gives me insight as to the way the company is run. For example, perhaps they sacrificed short-term earnings, by investing in a new distribution center that would generate huge savings three to five years out. This clearly shows me the company is not managing for the next quarter but the next decade. I repeat the analysis for each subsequent year until I review the latest published reports.

Public companies, by law, must disclose financial information as well as anything the company believes to be material to the running of the business. Recall that when you buy a stock, you are purchasing a piece of a business and are now a partner in that company. The annual report is a way for management to keep you updated on what happened in your company over the past year.

After I have read the letter to shareholders, there are usually a number of nice glossy pages on all the great things the company has done in the past year. Smiling employees, charts forever pointing higher, and pictures of products. That is the part I read through rather quickly. It gives a nice overview of what the company does, but for a more in-depth look, you need to read or at least skim the company's 10-K.

The 10-K is a report filed by the company at the end of their fiscal year with the Securities and Exchange Commission. It goes into much greater detail about the business, risk factors they face, legal proceedings, and executive compensation. If I have trouble understanding what the company does after reading about the business, I know this company is outside my field of competence.

In a recent read of the General Mills 10-K, I found that more than seven pages were devoted to explanations of their business. They provide a company overview of what they do, who they sell to, and how they break down their reporting (retail, international, and bakeries). They then list all the brands they sell in their retail division (cereals such as Cheerios, Lucky Charms, and Raisin Bran). In the international segment they manufacture their product in 17 counties and sell them in more than 100. In the bakery segment they sell to both retail and wholesale customers under the Pillsbury and Gold Seal labels. I also learned that demand for frozen baked goods and baking products is stronger in the fourth quarter. You can learn a tremendous amount about a company without leaving the comfort of your living room.

Management's Discussion

Usually toward the end of the annual report is the part I like best. It is called Management's Discussion and Analysis. Here management lays out the financial results and discusses very fine points of the business in order to give the shareholder an understanding of the story behind the numbers. The person who said, "God is in the details" must have been referring to this section of the annual report.

The most interesting part of management's discussion and analysis is what they put into the notes to consolidated financial statements, or *footnotes* for short. In the footnotes management explains in more detail significant accounting policies. In Procter & Gamble's 2005 annual report, note 1

footnotes provide details for the numbers that appear in the company's financial statements. Supposed to provide a better understanding of a particular number.

discusses in more detail the nature of the company's operations, how they came up with certain estimates, and what comprises selling, general, and administrative expenses, just to name a few points. For example P&G's sales for 2006 were $68 billion. As a shareholder you would want to know when P&G recognized those sales as revenue. If the customer ordered the goods months in advance but they were not shipped, did P&G count that as a sale? Or did they wait to get paid before they entered in their books as revenue?

By looking at the notes to the consolidated financial statements and reading the section titled Revenue Recognition, I found the answer. "Our policy is to recognize revenue when title to the product, ownership, and risk of loss transfers to the customer, which generally is on the date of shipment." Most footnotes are simple and easy to read and understand. Sometimes they are not.

I have a quick and fast rule when it comes to not understanding a footnote. If I read it a couple of times and still don't understand it, I call the investor relation department of the company and ask them to explain it to me. If I still don't understand it, I come to the conclusion that management doesn't really want average shareholders to understand it for one reason or another. That to me is a big warning sign. If management has something to hide, the footnotes are usually the place where they hide it.

Marty Whitman, co-chief investment officer of Third Avenue Management, believes that a company's filings must be understandable enough so that someone with an IQ of 70 will be able to interpret them. He invests in businesses only where he can appreciate excellent and clear filings.[17]

If the New York Stock Exchange gave a quiz on the annual report of the company prior to an investor buying the stock, I would bet dollars to donuts that investors would make much wiser decisions. Spend the time to read the reports and get a feel for management. You will learn much about the business and the management team, and this will give you the confidence to hold onto the stock when Mr. Market tries hard to frighten you into selling at a loss. A few hours of reading is not too big a price to pay when you are investing your hard earned money. The time it takes you to read the annual report will show up in higher balances in your brokerage account.

As critical as management is for the success of a company, you also need to watch another factor: competition. Great management running a buggy whip company in the early 1900s would not have been able to stem the tide of that declining industry. Buffett came to the conclusion that

> . . . with few exceptions, when management with a reputation for brilliance tackles a business with a reputation for poor fundamental economics, it is the reputation of the business that remains intact.[18]

In the next chapter I show you how to find companies that dominate their industries and leave the competition in the dust.

Key Points

1. Publicly available reports provide a type of "passive transparency." A lot of information is in the proxy statement, for example, about management compensation. Before you hand over your money, you should do some reading.

2. Some corporate managers comply with the reporting requirements, knowing full well that most people don't read them. But remember some compensation programs are schemes under which a few greedy executives siphon off *your* money to line *their* pockets. They comply, but you have to read to find out what they are doing.

3. When you examine a company, look for a manager's attributes, including the ability to make wise decisions, provide real leadership, and keep the business profitable. But above all else, you want to be sure management has honesty and integrity.

Chapter 6

Competition: Threat or Opportunity?

The Enduring Competitive Advantage

The difficulty never lies in identifying what a good business is today. The true difficulty is finding what will be a good business five or ten years down the road.[1]

—Jean-Marie Eveillard

While I was growing up, one of my best friends lived across the street. Ed was a sharp guy who went on to head up a foreign exchange trading desk at a major bank. We had become friends when I'd moved into the neighborhood at the age of six. During Ed's junior year in college, he was selected for a work-study program at a bank in Tokyo, Japan. Upon his return he shared with me the exciting world of foreign exchange trading and a food he had grown very fond of while living in Tokyo—sushi. "How could anybody eat raw fish?" I asked and Ed began to explain that once you acquired the taste, it grew on you.

That was back in the 1970s and I don't recall seeing a single sushi restaurant in Brooklyn, New York, at that time. When I walk out of my house today, I don't think I can drive half a mile in any direction without bumping into one. I am sure that when the first few sushi restaurants opened in Brooklyn, there were lines of people waiting to get in. As time went on and sushi became more popular, other restaurant owners saw the demand and started to open competing restaurants. In a short time the market became flooded with sushi restaurants and I now wonder how many of them are turning a profit.

Trends determine not only what kinds of businesses dominate, but also how long they are likely to remain in business. A business that relies too much on a trend and is slow to innovate and adapt does not stay in business too long. The average life span of a company in the S&P 500 index has gone from roughly 25 to 35 years in the 1950s to about 10 to 15 years today.[2] That should give you an insight as to how competitive the marketplace has become.

The Moat

The sushi story is not unique in business; in fact it is quite typical. A successful business breeds competitors who want to take a sliver of their profits and market share. Once a company dominates a certain industry, it seems everybody wants to get into the act. It happens when one or two companies dominate an industry, garner a large percentage of market share and, like day follows night, attract a large group of competitors. What was once a great business with large profit margins and virtually no competition is then faced with shrinking margins and competitors at every turn.

If a company is able to dominate its industry in the U.S. market, they are doing something very right. The United States is the greatest capitalist society the world has ever known. The United States share of total world output is 21 percent and has remained relatively constant for more than 30 years! The total U.S. output in 2002 was $10.3 trillion, more than the two next-largest economies, China and Japan, combined.[3] Yet the U.S. population makes up less than 5 percent of all the people on this planet. Another way of looking at it: Five percent of the world's population living in the United States produces 21 percent of the total world's output—a staggering statistic.

Companies that have a large part of the market share and are able to increase it have a competitive advantage within the industry. One of the criteria that Warren Buffett uses when buying a business is to analyze how big the company's competitive edge is. He even coined a phrase for it, the *economic moat*. He explained that in days of old, castles were protected by moats. When enemies tried to storm the castle, they had to not only contend with archers and catapults but also the moat that surrounded the castle. The wider the moat, the harder it was for the enemy to attack the castle.

I'm like a basketball coach, I go out on the street and look for seven-footers. If some guy comes up to me and says, "I'm five-six, but you ought to see me handle the ball," I'm not interested.[4]
—*Warren Buffett*

Buffett tries to buy businesses that have very wide economic moats around them. This makes it very difficult for competitors to try to take away market share. He also wants to know that management is continually increasing the size of the moat. The wider the moat the more protected the business, the narrower the moat the less defensible. As Buffett writes, "In business, I look for economic castles protected by unbreachable moats."[5]

You hardly ever hear Wall Street talking about the competitive advantage or the economic moat a company has, but the moat is vital to running the business successfully. As Buffett reminds us this is one of the most important secrets to investing:

> The key to investing is not assessing how much an industry is going to affect society or how much it will grow, but rather determining the competitive advantage of any given company and, above all, the durability of that advantage. The products or services that have wide, sustainable moats around them are the ones that deliver rewards to investors.[6]

economic moat
a term coined by Warren Buffett referring to the competitive advantage a company has over its competitors. The moat acts as a barrier against other companies trying to gain market share.

Before we go scouting for these large "economic castles protected by unbreachable moats," I want to share with you the different kinds of moats a company may have. By understanding the nature of the moat, you will then be able to easily recognize a company with a competitive advantage. Be aware that there is not an abundance of these types of companies in the market but finding and owning them is financially rewarding. Out of a database of 1,900 companies, Morningstar.com, a stock research web site and newsletter, identified only 189 companies as possessing an "unbreachable" or wide moat as of July 2007.

Types of Moats

Finding companies with a wide moat is a two-step process, half art and half science. For the art side, all you need to do is to see yourself as the customer and ask yourself why you would choose one product or service over another. There are basically four types of moats that keep customers loyal to a particular company.

Brand If your grocery store were out of Coke, would you buy Boca–Cola, even if it were $1 cheaper for a six-pack? Most people wouldn't, and that is what makes a powerful brand and great business. Each year BusinessWeek ranks the top 100 brands in the world (see Table 6.1). They also assign a dollar value to the strength of the brand. The most recognizable brand in the world is Coca-Cola. The value of their trademark alone is estimated at $67 billion.[7]

Rolex watches has built such a powerful brand that consumers pay for them in the tens of thousands of dollars, and on the other extreme, Timex watches can still be bought in drugstores for $29.95. Both watches deliver the same function; they tell time yet the Rolex brand conjures up images of power, success, and affluence. Rolex has a hefty advertising budget that continually supports the lifestyle the brand is trying to portray. Buffett said that if he was given $100 billion and told to take market share away from Coca-Cola, he would return the money. The competitive advantage of a brand is that consumers are willing to pay more for the product or service and many times won't accept any substitutes.

Switching A captive customer is a great customer to have. There are certain industries that make it difficult for a customer to switch from one provider to another. The nature of the product handcuffs the customer and keeps them locked into using the company's product or service.

If you woke up tomorrow morning and decided to switch the brand of socks you wear, there is not much to keep you locked into the old brand. However, you would probably not be so willing to switch your accounting software that

TABLE 6.1   The 10 Top Brands—2006

Rank	Company	Country of Ownership	2006 Brand Value ($ millions)
1	Coca-Cola	U.S.	$67,000
2	Microsoft	U.S.	$56,923
3	IBM	U.S.	$56,201
4	GE	U.S.	$48,907
5	Intel	U.S.	$32,319
6	Nokia	Finland	$30,131
7	Toyota	Japan	$27,941
8	Walt Disney Co.	U.S.	$27,848
9	McDonald's	U.S.	$27,501
10	Mercedes-Benz	Germany	$21,795

Source: *BusinessWeek,* The Top 100 Brands, August 7, 2006.

your company has been using for the past decade. Unless you were extremely unhappy, switching programs would be a major disruption for your employees and business. You would need to invest considerable time and money for your accounting department to get up to speed on the new program as well as to pray that your old data transfers over to the new system smoothly. That is the competitive advantage of providers that lock up the customer; it's too much of a nightmare to switch.

Besides computer software companies, medical replacement parts companies like Medtronic, Stryker, and Johnson & Johnson also lock up the customer. There is a big deterrent for doctors to switch products regardless of price. Think of how much time and training doctors invest in learning how to implant these products and you can appreciate the competitive advantage companies in this industry have. The time, energy, and risk associated with switching products is a preventive barrier that acts like handcuffs by keeping the end user chained to the product.

Cost When a company is in a business where the difference between products is difficult to distinguish (commodity industries like glass, steel, gasoline, etc.), the more efficient and low-cost producer has a competitive advantage. For example, since everyone who owns a car needs insurance, the only competitive edge car insurance companies have is price. GEICO has a competitive advantage in the car insurance industry because it sells direct to consumers and bypasses brokers. The savings GEICO gets from not paying commission to brokers is passed on to the consumer; hence they can offer lower prices than their competitors.

Forward Air Corporation offers an alternative for shippers to move cargo by ground instead of air via their 81 terminals across the United States. They handle more than 30 million pounds of cargo that needs to be expedited on a weekly basis. The company's network is so efficient that UPS, FedEx, and DHL use them to move some of their cargo. Since they do such large volume, they are able to reduce the cost per pound by distributing their expenses over their wide network of terminals, thereby having economies of scale.

Because Forward Air has lower costs, it would be very costly for a competitor to compete with them and replicate their network. That is why other companies use them instead of doing it themselves; they have perfected a more efficient, cost-effective way to move cargo. The cost, know-how, experience, and infrastructure of Forward Air act as deterrents to competitors.

Protection The Verrazano–Narrows Bridge is the largest suspension bridge in the United States, at 4,260 feet. It connects the boroughs of Staten Island and Brooklyn in New York City. Each day more than 200,000 vehicles cross the bridge and pay a toll. Imagine what a great business you would have if you would be able to own the bridge and collect the tolls. There are several types of businesses with a competitive advantage like that, due to patents, access to resources, or government protection.

When a pharmaceutical company comes out with a blockbuster drug, they have a patent on that drug for 17 years. That means the only place one can get Lipitor is from Pfizer. This patent has created a huge competitive advantage. In 2005 alone, Lipitor generated $12 billion in sales and was responsible for 24 percent of Pfizer's total revenue.

Florida Rock Industries sells and mines construction aggregates (rock, sand, and gravel used for building roads). They have mining aggregate permits issued by the states of Florida, Georgia, and Virginia. States do not give out permits very easily and over the past few years many municipalities stopped issuing permits, citing environmental concerns. A company with permits to mine aggregates is operating with an economic moat that makes it difficult for their competitors to take away market share.

When television was in its infancy, having a broadcast license was like having a license to print money. With only three networks, (CBS, NBC, ABC) companies had very few choices where to spend their advertising dollars. Competition was also limited since the Federal Communications Commission (FCC) was not giving out any more licenses. The three networks were the beneficiaries of FCC advertising restrictions for decades. Companies that have some type of protection are great businesses to own; however due to more competitive global markets and government regulations, they are becoming harder to find. See Table 6.2.

return on equity (ROE)
a measure of how profitable a company is. It is derived by dividing net income by total shareholder equity. ROE tells shareholders how effective management is in deploying their money. It is expressed as a percentage and makes comparison between different companies much easier.

net profit margin (NPM)
a measure of how profitable a company is after all expenses and taxes are paid. It is derived by dividing net income by total sales or revenue. It is expressed as a percentage and makes comparison between different companies much easier.

The Numbers Speak

Now that we can appreciate the unique position that a company with a competitive advantage has in attracting market share, let's see how the advantage plays out on the bottom line.

Two variables that can be found in a company's financial statement indicating to me that a company is a leader in their industry: *return on equity (ROE)* and *net profit margin (NPM)*. These two variables are the

TABLE 6.2 Companies that have a competitive advantage

Company	Description
3M	Makers of scotch tape, Post-its, and 50,000 other products. Products are sold in over 200 countries. Market leader in innovation and expertise in material sciences.
Bed Bath & Beyond	Market leader with over 800 stores nationwide selling bed linens, towels, cookware, and housewares. Over 800 big box retail stores nationwide.
Coca-Cola	World's largest beverage company. Manufactures and distributes major brands like Coca-Cola, Diet Coke, Sprite, and Minute Maid through bottlers around the world. Most recognized brand in the world.
Expeditors International	Logistics and freight forwarder with global network of offices in 150 cities on six continents.
Graco	Market leader in designing, manufacturing, and selling specialized pumps and spray guns, for the vehicular, construction, food, chemical, and plastics industries.
Harley-Davidson	The only major U.S. manufacturer of heavyweight motorcycles. Has over 1,000 dealers worldwide.
McGraw-Hill	Global information provider through brands like Standard & Poors, McGraw-Hill Education, *BusinessWeek*, and *Aviation Week*. Also owns four TV stations.
Medtronics	World's largest manufacturer of implantable biomedical devices, with sales to over 120 countries.
Paychex	Provider of computerized payroll–accounting services, tax return filing services, and other business services to more than 543,000 small- to medium-sized businesses in 36 states.
Thor Industries	Largest manufacturer of RVs and the largest builder of small- and mid-sized buses in North America. Manufactures wide range of motor homes and travel trailers in the United States and Canada through its Airstream, General Coach, and Dutchmen lines.

first numbers I look at when reviewing a company's financials. In the next two chapters I elaborate more on how to look at financial statements and explain what they mean in more depth, so don't worry if you don't catch it all here.

TABLE 6.3 Consolidated Balance Sheet		
The McGraw-Hill Companies Years ended December 31 (in thousands)	2005	2004
Total Assets	$6,395,808	$5,841,281
Total Liabilities	$3,282,660	$2,856,769
Total Shareholder's Equity	$3,113,148 (A)	$2,984,512 (D)

Source: McGraw-Hill 2005 Annual Report.

Return on Equity (ROE)

If a company truly has a competitive advantage over its competitors, then it should be earning higher profits. Consumers should be buying or using more of a company's product or service resulting in higher earnings.

One indicator that measures a company's profitability is return on equity (ROE). ROE is simply the return a company makes on the shareholder's equity. I show you how it is calculated, but many financial sites on the Internet already have the ROE calculated and prominently displayed. Also, most company annual reports feature the ROE within the first few pages in a chart or table.

ROE is derived from two different financial statements, Statement of Income and the Balance Sheet.

Table 6.3 shows the way the shareholder's equity appears in McGraw-Hill's Consolidated Balance Sheet, which can be found in the company's SEC 10-K filing and also in their 2005 annual report.

Table 6.4 shows how the net income appears in the company's Consolidated Statement of Income in McGraw-Hill's 2005 annual report.

TABLE 6.4 Consolidated Statement of Income		
The McGraw-Hill Companies Years ended December 31 (in thousands)	2005	2004
Net Income	$844,306 (B)	$755,823 (C)

Source: McGraw-Hill 2005 Annual Report.

Using this total Shareholder's Equity and Net Income data, we can quickly figure out McGraw-Hill's return on equity (ROE) for the past two years:

Return on Equity	2005: 27.1%	((B) $844,306/(A) $3,113,148)
	2004: 25.3%	((C) $755,823/(D) $2,984,512)

McGraw-Hill reported their ROE in 2005 of 27.1 percent, which means that they were able to earn a 27 percent return on the shareholder's equity of the company. If the management of McGraw-Hill were to convert total shareholder's equity to cash and deposited that in the bank, they could have earned about 4 percent in 2005. This should give you an idea how good a job management was able to do in 2005 to create a ROE of 27 percent.

McGraw-Hill's ROE is good compared to investing it in a bank account, but how well did they do against the competition? If McGraw-Hill does have a competitive advantage, then their ROE should be higher than the industry average. We also want to see if they just got lucky and had a good year or they were able to trounce the competition over time. Using a five year average of the ROE to lessen the chances of a company's having just one good year, we show the results in Table 6.5.

Calculating ROE

1. Take the net income (money that is left over after all expenses are paid) found on the Statement of Income.

2. Divide net income by total shareholders' equity (amount of assets owned by the company, minus all liabilities) found on the balance sheet.

3. The result is ROE (expressed as a percentage).

The numbers show that McGraw-Hill's ROE for 2005 was no fluke. Over the past five years they have averaged a 27 percent ROE. The average five-year ROE for the printing and publishing industry was only 8 percent, telling us that McGraw-Hill is an industry leader. A similar 5-year comparison for 10 leading companies that have a competitive advantage is revealing. See Table 6.6.

In addition to giving investors insight into the return a company is able to achieve on their shareholder's equity, ROE goes one step further. It is a convenient indicator allowing investors to compare companies side by side regardless of

TABLE 6.5 McGraw-Hill's ROE 2005			
Company	*5 Yr ROE*	*5 Yr ROE*	*Industry*
McGraw-Hill	27%	8%	Printing & Publishing

Source: www.reuters.com through 12/22/06.

TABLE 6.6 Return on Equity (ROE)			
Company	5 Yr ROE	5 Yr ROE	Industry
3M	31%	21%	Conglomerate
Bed Bath & Beyond	24%	14%	Retail–Specialty
Coca-Cola	33%	31%	Beverages
Expeditors Intl.	23%	22%	Transportation
Graco	45%	19%	Misc. Capital Goods
Harley-Davidson	29%	21%	Recreational Products
McGraw-Hill	27%	8%	Printing & Publishing
Medtronics	22%	19%	Medical Equipment
Paychex	29%	22%	Business Services
Thor Industries	23%	16%	Mobile Homes

Source: www.reuters.com through 12/22/06.

industry or size. Investors should focus on companies that produce high ROEs that have been trending higher over the past five years.

If a company achieves a high ROE that means they are increasing their net profit and the worth of the business (shareholder's equity). When the net worth of the business rises, shareholders will be rewarded with a higher share price.

Calculating Net Profit Margin

1. Take the Net income (money that is left over after all expense are paid).
2. And divide it by Net sales, also referred to as Revenue.
3. The result is Net profit margin (expressed as a percentage).

Net Profit Margin (NPM)

A business is not worth much if it can't turn a profit. The net profit margin is another good measurement of long-term value. Companies with competitive advantages should have higher than industry average net profit margins. The *net profit margin* is the percentage of profit earned for every dollar of sales. A company with a 13 percent profit margin means for every dollar of sales, the company was able to convert 13 percent of it to profit. The following table tells the whole story; companies with industry leading ROEs usually have industry leading net profit margins. See Table 6.7.

TABLE 6.7 Net Profit Margin (NPM)

Company	5 Yr NPM	5 Yr NPM	Industry
3M	13%	11%	Conglomerate
Bed Bath & Beyond	9%	7%	Retail–Specialty
Coca-Cola	21%	16%	Beverages
Expeditors Intl.	5%	3.5%	Transportation
Graco	16%	6%	Misc. Capital Goods
Harley-Davidson	15%	10%	Recreational Products
McGraw-Hill	13%	6%	Printing & Publishing
Medtronics	20%	11%	Medical Equipment
Paychex	26%	9%	Business Services
Thor Industries	5%	4%	Mobile Homes

Source: www.reuters.com through 12/22/06.

This five-year comparison makes a compelling case for the companies shown. All of them exceeded the five-year industry averages. You should look not only at the five-year average because averages smooth data and yearly changes can go unnoticed. For example, this is the way the net income and net sales appear in 3M's Consolidated Statement of Income, which can be found in their 2005 annual report.

Net profit margins are derived entirely from information found on the Statement of Income. See Table 6.8.

Using this net sales and net income data, we can quickly figure out 3M's net profit margin for the past three years:

	Net Profit Margin		
2005	15.1%	(B) $3,199/(A)	$21,167
2004	14.9%	(C) $2,990/(D)	$20,011
2003	13.2%	(E) $2,403/(F)	$18,232

TABLE 6.8 Consolidated Statement of Income

3M Company and Subsidiaries
Years ended December 31

(in millions, except per share amounts)	2005	2004	2003
Net Sales	$21,167 (A)	$20,011 (C)	$18,232 (E)
Net Income	$ 3,199 (B)	$2,990 (D)	$2,403 (F)

Source: 3M 2005 Annual Report.

Over the past three years, 3M was able to increase their net profit margin each year, a very strong showing. As an investor you want to see companies that have net profit margins that are trending higher.

Competitive Advantages Are Not Forever

Finding a company with a competitive advantage is only half the battle. The next step is to try to discern whether the competitive advantage will last. The business battlefield is a very treacherous place. When a company dominates its industry, competitors will work night and day trying to cross that moat and attack the castle. A battle has been taking place between companies in the field of portable media players for several years. On October 23, 2001, Apple Computer launched the iPod, a media player that can put "1,000 songs in your pocket." The iPod was an instant hit. Music lovers were suddenly able to download all their favorite albums into a small device, plug in their headphones, and have a library of music at their fingertips. The iPod has made CDs obsolete as you can now buy the songs you like from a web site (Apple's iTunes), download them to your iPod, and have them with you wherever you go. Sales and profitability rocketed for Apple after this product was introduced, and they held a tremendous share of this new industry—their economic moat was huge.

You could almost predict what happened next. The iPod attracted competitors like bees to honey. Competitors offered more memory, better features, and lower prices. Powerhouse companies such as Sony, Dell, and Microsoft tried to breach iPod's huge moat but were unsuccessful. iPod's moat continually widened as Apple came out with newer versions at lower prices. A multibillion dollar business has also grown around the iPod offering more than 3,000 peripherals like speakers, protective cases, and earbuds, further locking the consumer to the brand.

The consumer was also hooked on iPod not only for the features of the product but also for the "cool" factor, which made it very hard for the competition. Six years after its launch iPod's market share of the portable media player was more than 62 percent.[8] Apple is keenly aware that their competitors were hard at work trying to breach its moat, which is why Apple continually worked to expand it. But over the years, certain companies that once had a wide moat saw it diminish or vanish, for a variety of reasons.

What do the *New York Times*, CBS, and Kodak all have in common? At one time, each had a competitive advantage in its industry, but the advantage was not enduring. Each of these companies faced considerable challenges to its franchise over time. If you were an advertiser 20 to 30 years ago for a product used nationally, you had very few choices of where to air your ad. Today advertisers have many more choices (Internet, radio, cable television, magazines, etc.) than they had a generation ago, resulting in newspapers' and television networks' falling earnings.

A bit more than 30 years ago, Eastman Kodak's economic moat was very wide, almost as wide as Coca-Cola's. Kodak had "share of mind." Kodak, once one of the strongest brands in the world (Kodak's yellow box), has seen its print film sales plunge as more consumers switch to digital cameras. Whenever you wanted to take a picture of something important that you wanted to last a lifetime, you probably chose Kodak film. Try to think, besides Kodak, who else was there? The yellow box the film came in told you that Kodak was the best film there was, and you didn't want to fool around taking pictures of your baby's first steps with some cheap drugstore brand.

Over the past two decades something happened to Kodak's moat; it went from very wide to narrow. In 1984, Fujifilm paid for the rights to be the official sponsor of the 1984 Los Angeles Olympics, knocking out Kodak. The wide economic moat that Kodak had had for so long got smaller from that point on as consumers put Fuji and Kodak in the same quality class. In addition to their moat getting narrower, Kodak was late to the game in entering the digital revolution. As investors, the lesson we can learn from Kodak is that no matter how wide a company's moat, it has to be continually widened and never taken for granted. See Figure 6.1.

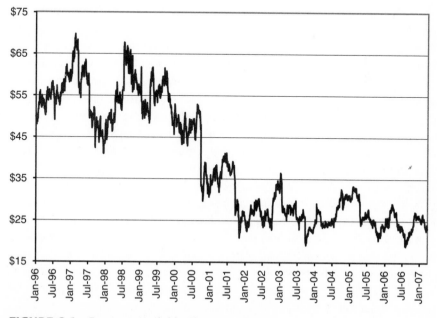

FIGURE 6.1 Eastman Kodak's Slumping Stock.

Another example of a competitive advantage that disappeared was in print editions of encyclopedias. Do you know anyone who recently bought a set of *Encyclopaedia Britannica* (price $1,700)? When I was in elementary school more than 35 years ago, every household had a set of encyclopedias. Only my wealthy friends had *Britannica*, which was more than an encyclopedia; it was a status symbol. Many of the contributors were world-renowned experts and Nobel Prize winners. All 32 volumes were handsomely bound and *Britannica's* 237 years of experience and reputation made it the gold standard. It had a competitive advantage that made it difficult for other encyclopedias to beat. But that advantage was not able to survive Microsoft's Encarta multimedia CD, which costs only $39.99, a fraction of *Encyclopaedia Britannica*. Encarta also happens to be the number one best-selling encyclopedia brand.[9]

The fight for market share and the ability to increase the size of a company's economic moat is going on each day and in almost every industry. When picking a company to buy, I try to see how a company will be able to widen their moat and keep competitors at bay. Who would have thought that the moats of newspapers would ever narrow? Yet that is exactly what happened, as the Internet became the first source readers go to for their news. This has hurt advertising revenue as major newspapers have seen sharp drops in readership. Television networks have also gone from wide-moat to narrow as cable television became a factor in most homes. Advertisers, which at one time had only ABC, NBC, and CBS to choose from, now can get their message across via cable stations with hundreds of competing channels.

Not much will happen to change the way people chew gum (Wrigley's), eat chocolate (Hershey's), or brush their teeth (Colgate) over the next 10 years. You will do well to invest in businesses with low probabilities of losing their competitive advantage, that can endure the next 10 to 20 years and beyond. It is very hard to figure out if a company in the telecommunications, Internet, or biotech industry will be able to maintain its competitive advantage over time, since these industries experience change at such a rapid rate.

Think of how hard it would be to take market share away from brands that have endured for generations. If you and I, for example, formed a partnership and decided to manufacture chewing gum, we would have a pretty tough time going head-to-head with Wrigley, a 115-year-old company with a share of the chewing gum market greater than 50 percent in the United States and close to 80 percent in some parts of Europe. Wrigley introduced a new brand of chewing gum, Orbit, in the United States in 2001. Due to the company's tremendous resources, brand name, efficiencies in productions, marketing—in other words, their competitive advantage—Orbit is now the number two brand in chewing gum in the United States. Not bad for an upstart brand. What chance would that leave our partnership in challenging Wrigley's market share?

Conclusion

Your first step when buying a company is to identify its competitive advantages and determine how enduring they are. Over time, they need to be able to weather economic storms better than their competitors while at the same time increasing shareholders' value. Once you identify those companies, keep up-to-date on their industries and corporate developments and monitor the size of their moat. Looking at the return on equity (ROE) and net profit margins (NPM) of the company once a year will tip you off to the size of the moat. Is it increasing or decreasing?

Wall Street doesn't spend much time looking at the competitive landscape or discussing the economic outlook for a company in a certain industry. Instead, it seems to focus on quarterly numbers, which to me represent nothing more than noise. Every business will have speed bumps and fall off into a ditch every now and then. Knowing that the companies you purchase have the edge, over time, will make all the difference in the world to your investment returns.

Investing in businesses with an enduring competitive advantage is one of the cornerstones of successful value investing. When you examine management and competition together, you have two of the four legs of the value table mastered. The remaining two are the financials and the price you pay for the stock. In the next two chapters, I show you how to look under the hood and analyze a company's financials. A strong financial statement tells you whether you are investing in a quality company.

Key Points

1. Quality companies are protected by economic moats, the all-important competitive advantage that makes it hard for competitors to gain market share. This economic moat is a concept worth remembering and applying in your analysis; even a good company without an economic moat won't last long.

2. There are basically four types of competitive advantages (economic moats):
   - Brand (Coca-Cola, for example, because Boca-Cola simply isn't the "real thing").
   - Switching (customer loyalty or the inability and unwillingness to go elsewhere).
   - Cost (dominating a commodity type industry through lower prices for the same or better value).

- Protection (ownership of a product or service that no one else is able to offer).
- Find out how enduring the competitive advantage is before investing.

3. Calculation of two ratios, return on equity (ROE) and net profit margin (NPM), are the first things to look for on a company's financial statement to get a clue about the company's competitive advantage. If these ratios are above industry averages and are trending higher, the company is worth pursuing further. If not, it's a waste of time.

The Essential Valuation Variables that Really Count

Financial Statement Basics

In 44 years of Wall Street experience and study, I have never seen depend-able calculations made about common stock values...that went beyond simple arithmetic or the most elementary algebra. Whenever calculus is brought in, or higher algebra, you could take it as a warning signal that the operator was trying to substitute theory for experience, and usually also to give speculation the deceptive guise of investment.[1]

—Benjamin Graham

E ven if you can't balance your checkbook, or failed every math test you took in high school, don't skim over this chapter! It's too important. If you are going to invest in businesses and you know your way around financial statements, you will have a big advantage. View this chapter like window shopping; spend a few moments looking at something and then move on. In fact, trying to dissect each number in the financial statements can sometimes work against you, as you can easily miss seeing the big picture.

You do not need to be an accountant to understand financial statements. If that was all that was needed to be a successful investor, then accountants would be on top of the Forbes 400 list of the wealthiest people in the world. The last I checked, I don't recall seeing many billionaires that listed "accountant" as their profession. Higher level math like calculus is also not required. Warren Buffett warned against doing math equations with "Greek letters" in them and said that "if calculus were required, I'd have to go back to delivering papers. I've never seen any need for algebra."[2]

Keep in mind that understanding financial statements is just one of the tools used in value investing. The goal is to use them to test the financial health of a business and the business' future earnings ability. You don't have to be an equestrian to be able to tell the difference between a thoroughbred capable of winning the Kentucky Derby and a carriage horse that clops around Central Park in New York City. Common sense and very basic math skills will help you navigate around this sea of numbers. In no time at all you will be able to look at a financial statement and tell the difference between a company with Triple Crown potential and an old mare headed for the glue factory.

I don't want to undermine the importance of reading financial statements; it's just not as complicated as most people might think. By putting in the time needed, you will give yourself an edge, which will ultimately lead to greater rewards.

Back of the Book

The majority of a company's annual report is made up of financial reports and their footnotes. Each year, management is required by law to disclose to shareholders certain financial information about the company. Most companies place a series of selected financial highlights in the beginning section of the annual report. Financial highlights are selected statistical data that showcase how well the company performed. Even if the company had a terrible year, there is always some piece of data they can extract to put a positive spin on a disappointing year. If sales and earnings were down, they might highlight lower expenses and tell you how they are watching the bottom line. They might highlight the increase in the advertising budget to demonstrate how marketing-focused they are.

Most of the time, financial highlights feature sales and earnings figures for the past two years. They may even throw in a few pie and bar charts to make the point on how well they are doing in a specific item like return on equity or profit margins. Take a quick peek at the financial highlights but nothing more. The really juicy stuff is in the back of the report. In my opinion, looking at the financial highlights is like watching a movie trailer; you're shown just enough to pique your interest but it sure doesn't replace watching the whole movie.

After all the nice pictures and glossy pages is a section entitled: Management's Discussion and Analysis of Results of Operations and Financial Condition. Don't let the long title scare you off because this is the most important part of the annual report. The SEC requires management to discuss past performance and to provide a thorough analysis of the company's financial position over the past three years. Specifically there are three areas that management must disclose: capital resources, liquidity, and results of operations.

This section is where you find the company's financial statements. The three reports are:

1. Consolidated statement of income.
2. Consolidated balance sheet.
3. Consolidated statement of cash flows.

Each report provides a different view of the company. By combining the information from them, shareholders are able to get a much clearer picture of the company's financial health.

Consolidated Statement of Income

The statement of income (or, income statement) gives an investor a view of the company over the course of a specific period of time. It tells you if the company is making money and how much they are making. The layout of income statements is fairly uniform; in other words if you've seen one, you've seen them all.

The top line of the income statement starts with the net sales or revenue, in other words the amount of gross income the company made during the period before any deductions. As you go down the income statement, it subtracts out costs and expenses. The net profit (or loss) is what is left after taking all the income and subtracting out the costs and expenses. One final note before we look at an actual income statement: "Income" doesn't really mean cash in the company's pocket. The way accounting rules work, companies can record income once the goods or services are sold, not when payment is received. If ABC Company listed $1 million as Net Sales on their income statement, that only means they sold $1 million, but did not necessarily receive payment for it. We will need to look at another financial statement to find where the movement of cash is recorded. More on this later.

The statement of income is usually presented in annual reports and 10-K filings showing the past three years. This allows investors to make comparisons between previous years and see how the company is doing. We use the statement of income for Coca-Cola for 2005, 2004, and 2003. I only want to point out the line item of importance and not bore you with accounting details.

TABLE 7.1 Coca-Cola's Net Operating Revenues		
2005	*2004*	*2003*
$23,104	$21,745	$20,857

Net Operating Revenue

The first line of the statement of income is Net Operating Revenue, or Net Sales. They both mean the same thing; the total amount of sales minus any goods returned and cash discounts provided to customers, for discounts and incentives.

Coca-Cola net operating revenues for the three years in this analysis, shown in millions of dollars (meaning the numbers are rounded off, often shown in reports as ($000). See Table 7.1.

By studying the past three years, you can easily see that Coca-Cola's revenues increased from $20.8 billion in 2003 to $23.1 billion in 2005. You can also figure out that 2005 revenue increased by $1.3 billion or 6.2 percent over 2004 (2005 revenue minus 2004 revenue divided by 2004 revenue), and 2004 revenue increased over 2003 revenue by 4.3 percent.

Net Income

Phil Fisher said: "All the sales growth in the world won't produce the right type of investment vehicle if, over the years, profits do not grow correspondingly."[3] The next important line item on the income statement is the net income, or the amount of money left over after paying out all costs, expenses, and taxes. See Table 7.2.

Coca-Cola had net income of $4.8 billion in 2005. Each shareholder earns a piece of the net income depending on how many shares they own. To find out how much of the $4.8 billion an owner of one share earns, divide the net income into the average shares outstanding, which comes out to $2.04 per share. See Table 7.3.

Coca-Cola's net income per share increased by .04 cents in 2005 (the difference between $2.00 in 2004 and $2.04 in 2005), or 2 percent. Net income per share increased from $1.77 in 2003 to $2.00 in 2004 for a gain of .23 cents, or 13 percent.

TABLE 7.2 Coca-Cola's Net Income over Three Years		
2005	*2004*	*2003*
$4,872	$4,847	$4,347

TABLE 7.3 How Much An Owner of One Share of Coca-Cola Earns

	2005	2004	2003
Net income	$4,872	$4,847	$4,347
Average shares outstanding	2,392	2,426	2,459
Basic net income per share	$2.04	$2.00	$1.77

There are three additional line items that are important to focus on when you are looking at the statement of income.

Sales Growth

A company that is not growing their sales or revenue will find it hard to grow their bottom line. Looking at sales growth over a one-year and five-year period does shed more light on the picture. In addition, also look at a company's sales growth in relation to the industry, sector, and the S&P 500 index. See Table 7.4.

The table shows that Coca-Cola's sales growth over a trailing 12-month (TTM) period versus a TTM of one year prior was 6.9 percent. The industry and sector Coca-Cola competes in had increases of 8.9 percent and 10.2 percent. The average of the S&P 500 index had sales increases averaging 15.9 percent. The five-year growth rate measures the sales growth over a longer period.

I tend to focus on companies that are able to grow their sales by at least 5 percent per year. In this case, Coca-Cola would make the cut and I would research why the company lagged behind the industry and sector. I would want to know if it was a temporary problem or something more serious.

Earnings Per Share (EPS) Growth

Earnings per share is another test of net income. You want to measure earnings per share over both a 12-month and a 5-year period. See Table 7.5.

Coca-Cola's earnings per share (EPS) for the trailing 12 months were 3.1 percent and 18.3 percent per annum over a 5-year period. Over the five-year

TABLE 7.4 Sales Growth over a One-Year and Five-Year Period

	Coca-Cola	Industry Beverages	Sector Consumer	S&P 500
Sales (TTM) vs. TTM 1 yr. ago	6.9%	8.9%	10.2%	15.9%
Sales 5 Yr. Growth Rate	5.9%	7.2%	8.1%	9.9%

Note: Growth rates are through February 2007.

TABLE 7.5   Earnings Per Share Growth

	Coca-Cola	Industry Beverages	Sector Consumer	S&P 500
EPS (TTM) vs. TTM 1 Yr. Ago	3.1%	14.8%	8.1%	23.3%
EPS 5-Yr. Growth Rate	18.3%	15.7%	12.2%	15.6%

Note: Growth rates are through February 2007.

period, Coca-Cola was able to outperform companies in their industry, sector, and the S&P 500 index.

When looking at EPS, I focus on companies that are growing EPS by a minimum of 10 percent per annum over a 5-year period. In this case Coca-Cola made the cut by increasing EPS by 18.3 percent.

Net Profit Margin (NPM)

What good is a business that increases sales and earnings and yet shows a loss? Perhaps they are not running a tight ship and let expenses creep up, eating away at profits.

As discussed in the previous chapter, the net profit margin is a good way to measure the percentage of profit that drops to the bottom line for every dollar the company sells.

In 2005 Coca-Cola produced net income of $4.8 billion on revenue of $23.1 billion. The net profit margin is nothing more than the percentage resulting when you divide the net revenue of $23.1 billion by the net income (profit) of $4.8 billion. This was 20.89 percent (rounding to 21 percent). For each dollar of revenue, Coca-Cola was able to capture 21 cents as net profit. That is a very significant amount of profit. By comparing the net profit margin of Coca-Cola over TTM and five-year average against its industry, sector, and S&P 500 index, we can conclude that the company is a market leader. See Table 7.6.

Look at net profit margin in relationship to the company's industry and sector. Certain industries tend to have small net profit margins and others high ones. I focus on companies that are above their industry's five-year NPM average.

TABLE 7.6   Net Profit Margin—Coca-Cola

	Coca-Cola	Industry Beverages	Sector Consumer	S&P 500
Net Profit Margin (TTM)	22.2%	17.1%	11.4%	13.7%
Net Profit Margin (5 Yr. Avg.)	21.4%	15.8%	10.7%	11.7%

Note: Growth rates are through February 2007.

	TABLE 7.7 Coca-Cola's NPM Showing Fluctuations		
Year	Net Revenue	Net Income	Net Profit Margin (NPM)
2003	$20,857	$4,437	20.8%
2004	$21,742	$4,847	22.9%
2005	$23,104	$4,872	21.1%

In this case, Coca-Cola with a 21.4 percent 5-year NPM average is far ahead of the industry's 5-year NPM average of 15.8 percent.

One of the first signs of trouble to be on the lookout for is declining NPM over a three-year period. This usually signals that:

- Competitors are gaining ground (the company is forced to lower prices).
- The company is not controlling expenses (higher expenses are eating into profits).
- The cost of materials to produce goods is rising (and rising costs means lower profits).

Coca-Cola's NPM fluctuated in the low 20s for the three years, which was very strong. See Table 7.7.

Summary

The Income Statement is the place you want the company to "show you the money." A quick checklist of three areas to review on the income statement is

1. Sales or Revenue Growth: Use a benchmark of five percent per year growth over the past three years as the minimum.
2. Earnings per Share Growth: Use a target of a 10 percent increase to EPS.
3. Net Profit Margin: This should be trending higher over the past five years and should be at or above the industry average over the same time period.

Balance Sheet

The balance sheet is found in the company's annual shareholder report and within the filing known as SEC Form 10-K. In addition, each quarter the company must file SEC Form 10-Q, which provides a balance sheet as of the close of the most recent quarter. The information that the balance sheet provides is a snapshot in time. It provides investors with information on the company's liquidity and solvency.

The balance sheet is divided into three parts:

Assets	Tells you what the company owns.
Liabilities	Tells you what the company owes.
Shareholder's Equity	Tells you what the company is worth.

Liquidity—Total Current Assets

The balance sheet is instrumental in telling investors how much assets the company has that is cash, or can be converted into cash very quickly. To make it even easier, in the assets section of the balance sheet, assets are listed from most liquid (cash) to least liquid (prepaid expenses and other assets). The heading Current Assets includes all assets that can be converted to cash within 12 months.

Coca-Cola's total current assets on December 31, 2005 were $10.2 billion, of which cash and cash equivalents (Treasury bills, CD's, etc. maturing in 90 days or less) totaled $4.7 billion. See Table 7.8.

Coca-Cola lists additional assets such as investments, property, plant and equipment, and a few more assets that when combined with the total current assets in Table 7.8 equal $29.4 billion. A summary of all of Coca-Cola's assets is shown in Table 7.9.

TABLE 7.8 The Coca-Cola Company and Subsidiaries Consolidated Balance Sheet		
	December 31 2005	*December 31 2004*
(in millions except par value)		
ASSETS		
CURRENT ASSETS		
Cash and cash equivalents	$ 4,701	$ 6,707
Marketable securities	**66**	61
Net accounts receivable	**2,281**	2,244
Inventories	**1,424**	1,420
Prepaid expenses and other assets	**1,778**	1,849
TOTAL CURRENT ASSETS	10,250	12,281

TABLE 7.9 Summary of Coca-Cola's Assets

	December 31 2005 (in millions)	December 31 2004 (in millions)
TOTAL CURRENT ASSETS INVESTMENTS	$ 10,250	$ 12,281
Equity method investments		
Coca-Cola Enterprises Inc.	1,731	1,569
Coca-Cola Hellenic Bottling Company S.A.	1,039	1,067
Coca-Cola FEMSA, S.A. de C.V.	982	792
Coca-Cola Amatil Limited	748	736
Other, principally bottling companies	2,062	1,733
Cost method investments, principally bottling companies	360	355
TOTAL INVESTMENTS	6,922	6,252
OTHER ASSETS	2,648	2,981
PROPERTY, PLANT, and EQUIPMENT—net	5,786	6,091
TRADEMARKS with INDEFINITE LIVES	1,946	2,037
GOODWILL	1,047	1,097
OTHER INTANGIBLE ASSETS	828	702
TOTAL ASSETS	$ 29,427	$ 31,441

Liquidity—Total Current Liabilities

Right below the assets the balance sheet reports Coca-Cola's liabilities, the total money the company owes. Total current liabilities for 2005 were $9.8 billion of which $4.4 billion were accounts payable (amounts owed to suppliers for goods or services that the company had not yet paid for at the close of the period). See Table 7.10.

The purpose of tracking the current assets and liabilities is to be able to discern the company's liquidity. A company that does not have enough current assets to meet their current liabilities could run into liquidity problems rather quickly. We want to make sure the company has at least $1 of current assets for every $1 of current liability. In our example, Coca-Cola has $10.2 billion of current assets against $9.8 billion of current liabilities of a current ratio of 1.04 (current assets of $10.2 billion/current liabilities of $9.8 billion). Once expressed as a ratio, it is much easier to compare one company to another. A current ratio of 1.04 tells us that the company has $1.04 in current assets for every $1.00 in current liabilities.

TABLE 7.10 Summary of Coca-Cola's Liabilities

	December 31, 2005	December 31, 2004
CURRENT LIABILITIES		
Accounts payable and accrued expenses	$ 4,493	$ 4,403
Loans and notes payable	4,518	4,531
Current maturities of long-term debt	28	1,490
Accrued income taxes	797	709
TOTAL CURRENT LIABILITIES	9,836	11,133

Investors should look at the current ratio over a period of three to five years to check whether the current ratio is trending higher (good), lower (not good), or was there a one-year fluke? Coca-Cola's current ratio over five years hovered around 1.00, so 2005 was right in line. See Table 7.11.

Solvency

The other financial information the balance sheet provides informs investors on the company's ability to pay off interest and principal on their long-term debt. If a company borrows a lot of money, it has to pay back the principal and interest. The balance sheet reveals whether the company is able to manage their debt.

As you go down the balance sheet, under Total Current Liabilities, you see that Coca-Cola's long-term debt was $1.1 billion at the close of 2005. On its own, $1.1 billion sounds like a lot of money so you need to measure the long-term debt in relation to shareholder's equity, the net worth of the business. Coca-Cola had long-term debt of $1.1 billion and shareholder's equity of $16.3 billion, so the debt to equity ratio was 7 percent ($1.1 billion of long-term debt/ $16.3 billion of shareholder's equity). The company had a very healthy business and generated a large amount of cash, so they had very little need to borrow

TABLE 7.11 Coca-Cola's Current Ratio 2001–2005

Year	Current Assets (in millions)	Current Liabilities (in millions)	Current Ratio
2001	$ 7,171	$ 8,429	0.85
2002	$ 7,352	$ 7,341	1.00
2003	$ 8,396	$ 7,886	1.06
2004	$12,094	$10,971	1.10
2005	$10,250	$ 9,836	1.04

money. Another way of looking at this ratio is to say that Coca-Cola has 93 cents of equity for every 7 cents in long-term debt.

A summary of the liabilities and shareholder's equity section of Coca-Cola's balance sheet is shown in Table 7.12.

Note that the total liabilities and shareholder's equity are identical to the total of all assets. The balance sheet is so named for two reasons. First, it summarizes the balances of the various asset, liability, and net worth accounts. Second, it summarizes the sum of liabilities and net worth balances with the sum of all assets.

Over the past five years, Coca-Cola's long-term debt has been decreasing while the shareholder's equity has been increasing. That is the reason the long-term debt to equity ratio (LT Debt/Equity) of the company has been decreasing over the past five years. In other words long-term debt represented a smaller percentage of Coca-Cola's worth. See Table 7.13.

I prefer companies that are able to fund their operations and expansion by way of cash generated from the business. This way they do not have any interest payments that will lower their profits or drain their cash flow. However some

TABLE 7.12 Summary of Liabilities and Shareholder's Equity—Coca-Cola		
	December 31, 2005 (in millions)	December 31, 2004 (in millions)
TOTAL CURRENT LIABILITIES	**9,836**	11,133
LONG-TERM DEBT	**1,154**	1,157
OTHER LIABILITIES	**1,730**	2,814
DEFERRED INCOME TAXES	**352**	402
TOTAL LIABILITIES	**13,072**	15,506
SHAREHOLDER'S EQUITY		
Common stock, $0.25 par value; Authorized—5,600 shares;		
Issued—3,507 and 3,500 shares, respectively	**877**	875
Capital surplus	**5,492**	4,928
Reinvested earnings	**31,299**	29,105
Accumulated other comprehensive income (loss)	**(1,669)**	(1,348)
Treasury stock, at cost—1,138 and 1,091 shares, respectively	**(19,644)**	(17,625)
TOTAL SHAREHOLDER'S EQUITY 16,355	**29,427**	15,935
TOTAL LIABILITIES and SHAREHOLDER'S EQUITY	**29,427**	31,441

TABLE 7.13 Coca-Cola's Long-Term Debt to Equity Ratio 2001–2005

Year	Long-Term Debt	Shareholder's Equity	LT Debt to Equity Ratio
2001	$ 1,219	$ 11,366	11%
2002	$ 2,701	$ 11,800	23%
2003	$ 2,517	$ 14,090	18%
2004	$ 1,157	$ 15,935	7%
2005	$ 1,154	$ 16,355	7%

companies do rather well when they can borrow money at low rates, invest it in their business, and return a handsome profit. Those are the types of companies we want to own.

A person that has run up a $10,000 credit card debt on clothing, vacations, and golf clubs, is being charged 18 percent finance charges and can barely make their monthly minimum payments is using debt poorly. On the other hand a person who took out a home equity mortgage of $100,000 at 7 percent and was able to invest that money and earn a 14 percent return was using debt wisely. The companies that are able to borrow long-term at very cheap rates and can generate high returns on their debt are using debt prudently. Long-term debt is not a bad thing when it comes to looking at the balance sheet. Sometimes it's not bad to owe money; it depends on the amount of debt as a percentage of shareholder's equity and the nature of the industry. We talk more about debt to equity ratio levels in the next chapter.

Summary

1. Overview: The balance sheet provides investors with a snapshot of how much liquidity a company has to meet its obligations and how well they can handle their debt.
2. Current ratio is a ratio of the amount of dollars of current assets to the amount of current liabilities (measure of liquidity).
3. Debt-to-Equity is a ratio of the amount of long-term debt a company has in relation to the shareholders' equity (measure of solvency).

Statement of Cash Flows

In my experience, the cash flow statement is the least read and understood of all the financial statements. Although it may look difficult, it really is a breeze

TABLE 7.14   Coca-Cola's Operating Activities 2003–2005

	Year Ended December 31 (in millions)		
	2005	2004	2003
OPERATING ACTIVITIES			
Net income	**$ 4,872**	$ 4,847	$ 4,347
Depreciation and amortization	**932**	893	850
Stock-based compensation expense	**324**	345	422
Deferred income taxes	**(88)**	162	(188)
Equity income or loss, net of dividends	**(446)**	(476)	(294)
Foreign currency adjustments	**47**	(59)	(79)
Gains on issuances of stock by equity investees	**(23)**	(24)	(8)
Gains on sales of assets, including bottling interests	**(9)**	(20)	(5)
Other operating charges	**85**	480	330
Other items	**299**	437	249
Net change in operating assets and liabilities	**430**	(617)	(168)
Net cash provided by operating activities	**$ 6,423**	$ 5,968	$ 5,456

once you understand what to look for. In a nutshell, the cash flow statement is a picture of the company's checkbook. It measures the flow of cash into and out of a company for a specific period of time. The time corresponds to the time period covered by the Statement of Income and also has the same ending date as the Balance Sheet.

The Statement of Cash Flows is three statements in one. It measures the cash flow of three different company activities.

1. *Operating Activities* measures the cash flow that went into and out of the company from day-to-day activities of the business. In the example of Coca-Cola, net cash provided by operating activities was $6.4 billion for 2005. This was the net cash that flowed in and out of the company from sales, payment of taxes and sales of assets among other line items. See Table 7.14.

2. *Investing Activities* measures the cash flow generated from the purchases and sales of assets, investment in plants and equipment, and other line items. The cash spent on property, plant, and equipment is referred to as capital expenditures or cap ex for short. This is cash needed for the company to maintain or expand the business. Large cap ex numbers

TABLE 7.15 Coca-Cola's Investing Activities 2003–2005

	Year Ended December 31 (in millions)		
	2005	2004	2003
INVESTING ACTIVITIES			
Acquisitions and investments, principally trademarks and bottling companies	(637)	(267)	(359)
Purchases of investments and other assets	(53)	(46)	(177)
Proceeds from disposals of investments and other assets	33	161	147
Purchases of property, plant, and equipment	(899)	(755)	(812)
Proceeds from disposals of property, plant, and equipment	88	341	87
Other investing activities	(28)	63	178
Net cash used in investing activities	(1,496)	(503)	(936)

one year could signal major investments that will hopefully pay off for the company in years to come. In 2005 Coca-Cola had cash outflows of $1.4 billion with $899 million in cap ex. See Table 7.15.

3. *Financing Activities* measures the activity of cash used to finance the company's cash flow: lines of credit, issuance of debt at low rates to institutions to pay off company debt at higher rates, are listed here. For 2005, the company had net cash outflows for financing activities of $6.7 billion. See Table 7.16.

Table 7.17 is the full Consolidated Statement of Cash Flows for Coca-Cola, summarizing three years' results as it appears in the company's annual report.

TABLE 7.16 Coca-Cola's Financing Activities 2003–2005

	Year Ended December 31		
	2005	2004	2003
FINANCING ACTIVITIES			
Issuances of debt	**178**	3,030	1,026
Payments of debt	**(2,460)**	(1,316)	(1,119)
Issuances of stock	**230**	193	98
Purchases of stock for treasury	**(2,055)**	(1,739)	(1,440)
Dividends	**(2,678)**	(2,429)	(2,166)
Net cash used in financing activities	**(6,785)**	(2,261)	(3,601)

TABLE 7.17   The Coca-Cola Company and Subsidiaries Consolidated Statement of Cash Flows

	Year Ended December 31 (in millions)		
	2005	2004	2003
OPERATING ACTIVITIES			
Net income	$ 4,872	$ 4,847	$ 4,347
Depreciation and amortization	932	893	850
Stock-based compensation expense	324	345	422
Deferred income taxes	(88)	162	(188)
Equity income or loss, net of dividends	(446)	(476)	(294)
Foreign currency adjustments	47	(59)	(79)
Gains on issuances of stock by equity investees	(23)	(24)	(8)
Gains on sales of assets, including bottling interests	(9)	(20)	(5)
Other operating charges	85	480	330
Other items	299	437	249
Net change in operating assets and liabilities	430	(617)	(168)
Net cash provided by operating activities	(A) 6,423	5,968	5,456
INVESTING ACTIVITIES			
Acquisitions and investments, principally trademarks and bottling companies	(637)	(267)	(359)
Purchases of investments and other assets	(53)	(46)	(177)
Proceeds from disposals of investments and other assets	33	161	147
Purchases of property, plant, and equipment	(B) (899)	(755)	(812)
Proceeds from disposals of property, plant, and equipment	88	341	87
Other investing activities	(28)	63	178
Net cash used in investing activities	(1,496)	(503)	(936)
FINANCING ACTIVITIES			
Issuances of debt	178	3,030	1,026
Payments of debt	(2,460)	(1,316)	(1,119)
Issuances of stock	230	193	98
Purchases of stock for treasury	(2,055)	(1,739)	(1,440)
Dividends	(2,678)	(2,429)	(2,166)
Net cash used in financing activities	(6,785)	(2,261)	(3,601)

(Continued)

	Year Ended December 31 (in millions)		
	2005	*2004*	*2003*
EFFECT OF EXCHANGE RATE CHANGES oN CASH AND CASH EQUIVALENTS	**(148)**	141	183
CASH AND CASH EQUIVALENTS			
Net increase (decrease) during the year	**(2,006)**	3,345	1,102
Balance at beginning of year	**6,707**	3,362	2,260
Balance at end of year	**$ 4,701**	$ 6,707	$ 3,362

After navigating the Statement of Cash Flows, you need to know one number that helps you separate businesses that are "cash cows" from businesses that are cash "hogs." That number is free cash flow (FCF). Free cash flow is the "show me the money" number. It is the cash left over after paying for all of the activities of the business and after making major capital expenditures. Free cash flow is determined by taking the net cash provided by operating activities minus capital expenditures.

Net cash provided by operating activities: (A) $6.423 million Investing Activities Purchases of property, plant, and equipment: (B) ($899 million) = Free Cash Flow of $5.524 million or $5.5 billion

Coca-Cola in 2005 produced a staggering $5.524 billion after paying all expenses and investments in new plants and equipments. In the next chapter I show you how to use free cash flow as a ratio to really find the "cash cows."

Key Points

1. The footnotes attached to a company's financial statements disclose some very important facts but most people don't bother with the fine print. This is a mistake.

2. The important and key ratios are not merely exercises in accounting. They provide you with the means for identifying quality companies and for eliminating the rest.

3. Liquidity is, literally, the lifeblood of a company. Without adequate cash, nothing gets done (not even the current bills can be paid). With enough cash, companies can, at the very least, keep current on their bills, and are also able to expand without having to go into debt.

Chapter

The Essential Operating Variables that Really Count

Bringing the Numbers to Life

Time is the enemy of the poor business and the friend of the great business.[1]
—Warren Buffett

When I was about eight years old, Grandpa Louie took my brother and me on our first fishing expedition. We were so excited that we hardly slept the night before. My brother and I woke up at the crack of dawn, grabbed the peanut butter and jelly sandwiches Mom had made the night before, and waited anxiously for Grandpa Louie's car to pull up in front of our house.

It was so exciting, going to the bait and tackle shop and buying blood-worms by the boxful. By far the most exciting part was following Grandpa Louie to his favorite fishing hole. We walked past the big party boats, past the old men fishing from the pier, and ended up in a small out-of-the-way place. Grandpa Louie turned to us and said, "If you're going fishing, you gotta know where to drop your line." At the end of the day, we all walked back to the car, exhausted and triumphant, holding two bucketsful of flounder. I didn't realize until recently that I had been taught a very important lesson on investing that day.

107

This lesson is worth remembering when you begin to select stocks. It *does* matter where you "drop your line," so to speak. Where do you invest? That's the question. It's not enough to know how to read and interpret financial statements, and you certainly would not want to undertake the task of reviewing hundreds of companies—just the thought of that could be overwhelming. One place you should start is right where you stand. Look around you and make a note of all the things you use every day, and you will find many great companies staring you right in the face.

In your daily routine, you come in contact with dozens of public companies and never have given them a second thought. When you woke up this morning and brushed your teeth with Crest toothpaste, took a shower and used Ivory soap, and washed your hair with Herbal Essence, Procter & Gamble (PG) was very happy.

When you came to the breakfast table and had a hot bowl of Quaker Oats, you could thank Pepsico (PEP). If you drove to the gym in your Mustang convertible (Ford Motor Co., F) insured by GEICO (Berkshire Hathaway, BRK.A), drank a Diet Sprite (Coca-Cola, KO) and ran on the treadmill in your Air Structure Triax sneakers (Nike, NKE) while listening to your iPod (Apple, APL), you came into contact with six more publicly traded companies. And I didn't even get to your lunch at Panera Bread Company (PNRA), checking your e-mail on your laptop (Dell, DELL), followed by an iced Café Mocha at Starbucks (SBUX).

Start your research for great companies by reviewing your day. What did you like about their products? Why did you purchase them? Would you recommend them to a friend? Most of the companies previously mentioned are in easy to understand businesses, with excellent brand recognition. Call the company or visit their website, get their annual report, and start reading. If you limit your investment universe just to companies whose products you use in your daily affairs, you will have a large group of companies to follow.

Another more mechanical approach is to look through a stock guide and find companies with great financials. Value Line Investment Survey lists close to 1,700 stocks that fall into 100 different industries. With so many industries to choose from, what are you to do? This survey provides the first stop you can use to reduce the size of the list. Right off the bat, many industries should be avoided because they comprise low-margin, highly competitive businesses that have low return on equity. As a starting point, you should want to invest in companies that are in industries that have the wind at their back—not in industries on the verge of extinction. In the previous chapter, I showed you how to study the numbers on the financial statements in comparative terms. Now I show you how to narrow down your list of potential value companies by comparing industries.

Whichever path you choose to begin your research, keep this in mind: Stick to your circle of competence. You will certainly understand certain industries and companies better than others. Stick with those you can understand and have a higher degree of confidence in. If, for example, you are the purchasing agent for your company and have a great experience with a vendor that happens to be a publicly traded company, right off the bat you are starting with a lot more knowledge about the company, industry, products, competitive advantage, management, and so on than the average investor. If you don't have an edge, then you are competing against somebody who does. Buffett has said that a simple and understandable business is one that lies within your circle of competence. He reminds investors that: "You only have to be able to evaluate companies within your circle of competence. The size of that circle is not very important; knowing its boundaries, however, is vital."[2] Stick to what you are familiar with and you will have a lot more confidence in your selections.

When you do define your circle of competence, stay within industries that are growing and have favorable economics. There are a variety of economics within each industry that better illustrate what I mean. I compare the different industries by using their operating margins, net profit margins, and return on equity (ROE). Why these three criteria? I have found that they are highly informative about the financial strength of a company. As Marty Whitman, an outstanding value investor and founder of Third Avenue Management said, "Based on my own personal experience—both as an investor in recent years and as an expert witness in years past—rarely do more than three or four variables really count. Everything else is noise." Since accounting is the language of business, it is vital to be able to understand certain accounting terms in order to value a business. I give you a glimpse at what I look for in a company's financials before investing.

Operating Margin

The first item is the company's operating margin. In a nutshell, it tells me how much of every dollar in sales or revenue the company has left after paying all the costs of running the business. It subtracts items such as the cost of goods sold and general and administrative expenses (rent, electricity, payroll, etc.) from revenue.

Let's say you and I form a 50/50 partnership and we go into the business of selling antique pocket watches on eBay. At the end of our first month I tell you we sold $10,000 worth of pocket watches. You then ask for your cut and expect $5,000 or 50 percent of our $10,000 in sales. But before I can give you your share, we need to subtract our cost of goods (pocket watches cost $6,000) and

TABLE 8.1 Operating Income of $1,500 or a 15 Percent Operating Margin	
Sales	$10,000
Less: Cost of Goods Sold	(6,000)
Gross Profit	$ 4,000
Less: General & Administrataive Expenses	(2,500)
Operating Income	$1,500
Operating Margin	**15%**

our general and administrative expenses (eBay fees, transactions fees, computer programmer, etc.), which come to $2,500. Table 8.1 breaks down how we get our operating margin.

I prefer to invest in businesses that have high operating margins. Businesses with low operating margins do not have much wiggle room when they need to be flexible on prices or when their costs rise. All it would take is a small bump in the road, and a business with a low operating margin can quickly sink into the red.

Net Profit Margin

The second criterion, net profit margin, is defined as the amount the company earned after all expenses including taxes (in other words, the bottom line), divided into the sales or revenue expressed as a percentage. In our pocket watch business, if our operating income was $1,500 and our taxes and all other expenses amounted to $500, our net profit would then be $1,000 and our net profit margin would be 10 percent. Great businesses have high net profit margins, and mediocre and bad businesses have low ones.

Return on Equity (ROE)

If you have a business that's earning 20%–25% [return] on equity, time is your friend. But time is your enemy if your money is in a low return business.[3]
—*Warren Buffett*

	Operating	Net Profit	
Operating Industry	Margin	Margin	ROE
Air Transport	9.2%	1.9%	12.5%
Electronics	5.8%	2.6%	7.0%
Auto Parts	7.0%	2.5%	12.5%
Medical Supplies	12.5%	7.3%	21%
Beverages (Alcoholic)	24%	12.5%	25%

TABLE 8.2 Industry Names

As of December 2006.

The third criterion, ROE, tells me how well management is handling the assets they have to work with and how much they have earned (in percentage terms) for the stockholders. ROE also allows investors to compare the profitability of any company, regardless of its industry by comparing ROE. There are several ways to figure out ROE, but for simplicity's sake, the formula that we use here is to divide the net profit into the shareholder equity (the net worth of the company). Once again, great businesses have high ROEs and bad businesses have low ones.

Now let's compare different industries and see how they stack up against each other (Table 8.2).

Before we analyze the numbers, I want to share with you an insight from a friend who has made his living betting on horses at the track. He said his secret was that he didn't pick winners; instead, he eliminated the losers. If a race had 10 horses, he would cross out the horses with the least probability of winning. On average, he would narrow down the horses in a race to four that had a high probability of winning. By doing so, he increased his chances of success from picking 1 in 10 to 1 in 4.

Using that logic allows us to eliminate industries in which we would not want to invest. The Air Transport and Electronics industries stand out as eyesores. The air transport industry has been plagued by price wars and soaring fuel costs. Several of the big carriers, including Delta and Northwest, filed for bankruptcy. The electronics industry has seen demand weaken for electronic components, especially in the telecommunications industry. Sony, Philips, Arrow, and Cubic Corporation all have seen their margins come under pressure. No matter how good management is, it is going to be extremely difficult to make money in an industry that works on very low net profit margins and has an ROE that is nothing to write home about. It's kind of tough to make money in an industry that has too many headwinds.

The Auto Parts industry is a pass, too. With low net profit margins and a mediocre ROE, I would be concerned that low selling prices and intense competition to only a few vendors could wipe out profits in a heartbeat. Once again, unless a company really stood head and shoulders above others in the Auto Parts industry, I would tend to avoid it. Over the next several years this industry will consolidate but until then it is too much of a crap shoot for my taste.

Now we are left with two industries, Medical Supplies and Beverages (Alcoholic). Both have price flexibility as pointed out by their high operating margins and net profit margins. In addition they are in industries that have very high ROEs. I would therefore begin my research with companies in those industries.

Companies such as Medtronics and Johnson & Johnson in the medical supplies industry have a large market share in implantable devices, defibrillators, and stents. Alcoholic beverage producers such as Anheuser-Busch and Constellation Brands might be in a bit of a funk right now, but they are excellent businesses in a good industry. Knowing in which pond to drop your fishing line, while not a guarantee of success, will increase your odds of earning a good return on your investment.

A Checklist

In the previous chapter I showed you a detailed breakdown of Coca-Cola's financial statements. By the end of this chapter you will be able to look at any company's financials and tell the difference between a healthy and a sickly company. You don't need to be an accountant to make that distinction. You also don't need to master every detail of the financial statement, just the parts that I show you. Many investors get bogged down in too much detail and sometimes miss the big picture. Keep in mind there is a lot more to reading a financial statement than I am showing you. If you want to learn more about the subject, I have listed several good books in the Resources section. For now, I want to give you what I have found to be the "must knows" of financial statements. I like to look at them with Henry David Thoreau's words in mind: "Our life is frittered away by detail . . . simplify, simplify, simplify!"

I now analyze three of the four financial statements of PepsiCo, Inc. All of the statements I use come from the company's 10-K, and I didn't leave anything out. The way you see the information here is the way they appear in the filing. The easy part of reading the financial statements, as I have said previously, is that they are pretty uniform; every company follows the same format. They're like traffic lights in the United States: green, yellow, and red are always in the same spots and mean the same thing. After reading this chapter a few times, I challenge you to go to the SEC's web site and search for any company's 10-K. You will be surprised at how familiar you are with the information.

Statement of Income: Operating and Net Profit Margins

As I said in the previous chapter, the statement of income is basically a scorecard for a specific period of time. It tells you how much the company's sales were, what it cost to get those sales, and how much was left over.

One of the key ratios I am concerned with is the net profit margin (NPM). This number, expressed as a percentage, tells you what percent of every dollar drops to the bottom line. As a general rule, companies with large NPMs have more room to weather financial storms than companies with razor-thin NPMs. Companies with large NPMs also have more cushion to absorb mistakes and adverse market conditions than those with small NPMs.

The Formula for Operating Margin Is:

> (2a) operating income ÷ (1) net revenue for PepsiCo, Inc., as of December 31, 2005(in $ millions): $6.3 billion ÷ $32.5 billion = 19.4% operating margin.

The Formula for Net Profit Margin Is:

> (2) net income ÷ (1) net revenue for PepsiCo, Inc., as of December 31, 2005(in $ millions): $4.0 billion ÷ $32.5 billion = 12.5% net profit margin. See Table 8.3.

Statement of Cash Flows

Cash flow is the lifeblood of every business. Without it, the rent doesn't get paid and the lights get shut off. The Statement of Cash Flows gives you a look into how much money flowed into and out of the company over a specific period of time.

I prefer to focus on free cash flow, which tells you how much cash actually fell to the bottom line. I learned this lesson when I was twenty-one years old working for my father. Dad manufactured ladies wear, which is a treacherous business requiring ample cash to pay contractors, suppliers, and overhead. At the end of one good year in business and no cash in the bank, my father called his accountant and asked him how the financial statements showed the business making a $100,000 profit, yet my father didn't have enough money to buy new equipment for the cutting room. "Where is the profit?" my father shouted into the phone. The accountant responded, "Hanging on your racks." A business can generate earnings but if the earnings are needed to further fund business growth

TABLE 8.3 PepsiCo, Inc. and Subsidiaries	
Consolidated Statement of Income	
Fiscal years ended December 31	
(in millions except per share amounts)	**2005**
(1) Net Revenue	**$32,562**
Cost of sales	**14,176**
Gross profit	**18,386**
Selling, general, and administrative expenses	**12,314**
Amortization of intangible assets	**150**
Restructuring and impairment charges	—
Merger-related costs	—
Operating Profit	**$5,922**
Bottling equity income	**557**
Interest expense	**(256)**
Interest income	**159**
(2a) Income from Continuing Operations before Income Taxes	**$6,382**
Provision for Income Taxes	**2,304**
Income from Continuing Operations	**$4,078**
Tax Benefit from Discontinued Operations	—
(2) Net Income	**$4,078**
Net Income per Common Share—Basic	
Continuing operations	**$2.43**
Discontinued operations	—
Total	**$2.43**
Net Income per Common Share—Diluted	
Continuing operations	**$2.39**
Discontinued operations	—
Total	**$2.39**

or pay the current bills, it is a phantom number that you can never hear jingle in your pocket.

The formula for free cash flow is:

(3) Net cash provided by operating activities − (4) capital spending

For PepsiCo, Inc., as of December 31, 2005 (in $ millions): $5.8 billion − $1.7 billion = $4.1 billion of free cash flow. See Table 8.4.

TABLE 8.4 Consolidated Statement of Cash Flows

PepsiCo, Inc. and Subsidiaries

Fiscal years ended December 31

(in millions)	2005
Operating Activities	
Net income	$4,078
Adjustments to reconcile net income to net cash provided by operating activities	
Depreciation and amortization	1,308
Stock-based compensation expense	311
Restructuring and impairment charges	—
Cash payments for merger-related costs and restructuring charges	(22)
Tax benefit from discontinued operations	—
Pension and retiree medical plan contributions	(877)
Pension and retiree medical plan expenses	464
Bottling equity income, net of dividends	(411)
Deferred income taxes and other tax charges and credits	440
Merger-related costs	—
Other noncash charges and credits, net	145
Changes in operating working capital, excluding effects of acquisitions and divestitures	
Accounts and notes receivable	(272)
Inventories	(132)
Prepaid expenses and other current assets	(56)
Accounts payable and other current liabilities	188
Income taxes payable	609
Net change in operating working capital	337
Other	79
(3) Net Cash Provided by Operating Activities	5,852
Investing Activities	
Snack Ventures Europe (SVE) minority interest acquisition	(750)
(4) Capital spending	(1,736)
Sales of property, plant and equipment	88
Other acquisitions and investments in noncontrolled affiliates	(345)
Cash proceeds from sale of PBG stock	214
Divestitures	3
Short-term investments, by original maturity	

(Continued)

TABLE 8.4 Consolidated Statement of Cash Flows (*Continued*)

More than three months—purchases	(83)
More than three months—maturities	84
Three months or less, net	(992)
Net Cash Used for Investing Activities	**(3,517)**
Financing Activities	
Proceeds from issuances of long-term debt	$25
Payments of long-term debt	(177)
Short-term borrowings, by original maturity	
More than three months—proceeds	332
More than three months—payments	(85)
Three months or less, net	1,601
Cash dividends paid	(1,642)
Share repurchases—common	(3,012)
Share repurchases—preferred	(19)
Proceeds from exercises of stock options	1,099
Net Cash Used for Financing Activities	**(1,878)**
Effect of exchange rate changes on cash and cash equivalents	(21)
Net Increase/(Decrease) in Cash and Cash Equivalents	436
Cash and Cash Equivalents, Beginning of Year	1,280
Cash and Cash Equivalents, End of Year	$1,716

Balance Sheet

The balance sheet shows how much a company owns (assets) and how much it owes (liabilities). The balance sheet also tells you how liquid and solvent the company is.

Liquidity: Current Ratio

A company is in a sound position when they have more current assets than current liabilities. This measure indicates that they should not have a problem in taking care of current liabilities that come due.

The formula for current ratio is:

(5) total current assets ÷ (6) total current liabilities

For PepsiCo, Inc., as of December 31, 2005 (in $ millions): $10.4 billion ÷ $9.4 billion = 1.11 current ratio. See Table 8.5.

Solvency: Long-Term Debt/Equity

Companies usually run into trouble when they have more debt than they can handle. The long-term debt-to-equity ratio measures the amount of long-term debt the company has as a percentage of the equity of the business. If a company has no long-term debt, then the ratio would be 0 percent. If a company has long-term debt equal to its equity, then the ratio would be 100 percent.

The formula for long-term debt/equity (LT debt/Equity) is:

> (7) long-term debt obligations ÷ (8) total common shareholder's equity

> For PepsiCo, Inc., as of December 31, 2005 (in $ millions): $2.3 billion ÷ $14.3 billion = 16% LT debt/equity.
> See Table 8.5.

Crossovers

Two more ratios of key importance are found on two different financial statements.

Return on Equity (ROE)

There are several great value investors who consider ROE the most important measure of a quality business. This is my "deserted island" indicator. If I could have only one piece of information about a company, I would want to know the ROE. Businesses able to earn high return on their equity have a unique position in their industry and/or superior management. The only difference between the ROE and the return on capital (ROC), is that the ROC includes the company's debt, which would increase the denominator, when you are making the calculation. The ROE and the ROC will be the same for a company that has no debt.

> *The single most important indicator of a good business is its return on capital. We believe that in almost every case in which a company earns a superior return on capital over a long period of time it is because it enjoys a unique proprietary position in its industry and/or has outstanding management.*
> *—Bill Ruane, Ruane, Cunniff & Co., Inc.*

TABLE 8.5 Consolidated Balance Sheet

PepsiCo, Inc. and Subsidiaries

December 31

(in millions except per share amounts)	2005
ASSETS	
Current Assets	
Cash and cash equivalents	**$1,716**
Short-term investments	**3,166**
	4,882
Accounts and notes receivable, net	**3,261**
Inventories	**1,693**
Prepaid expenses and other current assets	**618**
(5) Total Current Assets	**10,454**
Property, plant, and equipment, net	**8,681**
Amortizable intangible assets, net	**530**
Goodwill	**4,088**
Other nonamortizable intangible assets	**1,086**
Nonamortizable Intangible Assets	**5,174**
Investments in Noncontrolled Affiliates	**3,485**
Other Assets	**3,403**
Total Assets	**$31,727**
LIABILITIES and SHAREHOLDERS' EQUITY	
Current Liabilities	
Short-term obligations	**$2,889**
Accounts payable and other current liabilities	**5,971**
Income taxes payable	**546**
(6) Total Current Liabilities	**9,406**
(7) Long-Term Debt Obligations	**2,313**
Other Liabilities	**4,323**
Deferred Income Taxes	**1,434**
Total Liabilities	**17,476**
Commitments and Contingencies	
Preferred Stock, no par value	**41**
Repurchased Preferred Stock	**(110)**
Common Shareholder's Equity	
Common stock, par value 1.67¢ per share (issued 1,782 shares)	**30**

(Continued)

TABLE 8.5 Consolidated Balance Sheet (*Continued*)	
Capital in excess of par value	614
Retained earnings	21,116
Accumulated other comprehensive loss	(1,053)
	20,707
Less: repurchased common stock, at cost (126 and 103 shares, respectively)	(6,387)
(8) Total Common Shareholder's Equity	14,320
Total Liabilities and Shareholders' Equity	$31,727

Source: Statement of Income and Balance Sheet.
The formula for ROE is:

> (2) net income ÷ (8) total common shareholder's equity

> For PepsiCo, Inc., as of December 31, 2005 (in $ millions): $4.0 billion ÷ $14.3 billion = 28.5% ROE.

Free Cash Flow As a percent of Revenue

For most companies, a large percentage of reported earnings are ploughed back into the business to maintain plant and equipment. Looking at the free cash flow as a percent of revenue tells investors how much revenue actually gets turned into cash. Companies able to generate a large portion of their earnings in cash can either distribute the cash to investors by way of dividends or by buying back shares, or invest the cash to generate higher returns.

Source: Statement of Cash Flows and Statement of Income.
The formula for Free Cash Flow (FCF) as a percent of Revenue is:

> Free cash flow [(3) net cash provided by operating activities − (4) capital spending net income] ÷ (1) Net Revenue.

> For PepsiCo, Inc., as of December 31, 2005 (in $ millions): [$5.8 billion − $1.7 billion] = $4.1 billion ÷ $32.5 billion = 12.6% FCF as a percentage of revenue.

This analysis is the basic exercise you need to go through to identify the value of a company. It may seem obvious that you would want to pick a company with better numbers, in an industry that's above average. But as obvious as this might seem, people continue to pick stocks based on benchmarks like price per share, which don't tell much, rather than the more sensible *value* per share.

Here is a quick summary of the key variables:

1. 12.5% net profit margin
2. 19.4% operating margin
3. 28.5% ROE

Without looking at the average of the beverage industry, the numbers are looking very good. Both margins are in double digits and the business is able to produce a very high ROE.

1. 1.11 current ratio
2. 16% LT debt/equity
3. $4.1 billion of free cash flow
4. 12.6% FCF as a percentage of revenue

In terms of the ability of the company to meet current obligations, the level of LT debt and the high free cash flow, Pepsico is a company worth researching further.

In the next chapter, I compare and contrast these two methods to further make the case for more intelligent analysis.

Key Points

1. When you pick stocks of companies you already understand, you're off to a good start. Stick to your "circle of competence" and understand that circle's boundaries.

2. Companies with relatively high operating margins have superior flexibility. When prices rise and competition gets fierce, that high margin helps companies survive.

3. Pick leading companies in industries with better than average net profit margins, operating margins, and return on equity (ROE). This tells you that the company is in a good industry and/or management must be doing something right.

Chapter

The Price of Stock versus the Value of the Company

Basically, price fluctuations have only one significant meaning for the true investor. They provide him with an opportunity to buy wisely when prices fall sharply and to sell wisely when they advance a great deal. At other times he will do better if he forgets about the stock market and pays attention to his dividend returns and to the operating results of his companies.[1]

—Benjamin Graham

I t always made perfect sense to me to stock up on items that I use often, and with five growing children, that is a pretty long list. I am lucky to have a wife who puts up with my bulk buying and allows me to store all my provisions in a section of the basement. In my storage room you will find four dozen toothbrushes, 96 rolls of toilet paper, and a dozen tubes of toothpaste. By the way, those are just a few of the items I stock up on. Most people enjoy Sunday afternoons, lying back and just taking it easy. For many, that might mean sitting in front of the TV watching sports, spending time with the kids or grandchildren, or just taking a stroll around the mall. I sometimes do all the above, but most of the time you can find me in one of the various warehouse clubs looking for bargains. I can't seem to help it. I hate paying full price for anything, and that certainly includes items I use every day such as toilet paper, toothpaste, and paper towels.

In addition to saving money by purchasing in bulk, I find that many times the warehouse clubs offer coupons and I save even more. I really get excited when the manufacturer offers rebate checks on products I use most often. There is nothing like opening my mailbox and getting rebate checks for $10, $15, and sometimes $20 for products I was buying anyway. It really is found money. I can never understand why consumers would pay retail for, and buy at such high prices, products they use on a daily basis. It seems like such a waste of money. To sum up, I like a bargain and buy even more when prices are lower.

What does this have to do with investing? you might be asking yourself. In a nutshell—everything. What makes perfect sense in the real world gets lost many times when applied to investing. So sit back, grab yourself a nice hot cup of tea, and allow me to share with you my view of buying low and selling high when investing in stocks.

Lower Prices

I want to give you a very silly example, not to insult your intelligence but to make a rather obvious point. If you plan on brushing your teeth for the rest of your life and like one particular brand of toothpaste, would you wish for higher or lower prices for toothpaste? If you enjoyed eating spaghetti and were not the manufacturer, would you want prices to be higher or lower each time you shopped at the supermarket? These questions are similar to the ones Warren Buffett asked investors in his shareholder letters in 1987 and again in 1997.

The questions answer themselves; of course, you would want lower prices. When prices get really low, because of a sale or manufacturer's special, I am sure you would stock up on an item because you were able to get it at a good discount. Now let's get out of the real world and go to the world of investing. I want to share with you how this type of thinking is not so widespread.

> *"The investor with a portfolio of sound stocks should expect their prices to fluctuate and should neither be concerned by sizable declines nor become excited by sizable advances. He should always remember that market quotations are there for his convenience, either to be taken advantage of or to be ignored. He should never buy a stock because it has gone up or sell one because it has gone down."*[2]
> —*Benjamin Graham*

If you are a *long-term investor* (10-year-plus time horizon) in the stock market, would you welcome lower prices on your stocks over the next three years? Logically, most investors will respond, "Of course." However the way they act is at times totally opposite to this logic. Many investors become happy, and even euphoric, when stock prices rise over the short term. It gives them a great feeling to flip open the newspaper or click on the Internet and see their stock price moving higher. More times than not, they would use that opportunity to add to their position. In effect, they would welcome the idea of paying higher prices for toothpaste or spaghetti. The opposite happens when they see their stock prices fall. They get depressed, put on a long face, and mope around for the rest of the week.

For you as a long-term investor, lower prices over the short term should be seen as a manufacturer's rebate or store special. Only those who are going to sell their shares in the very near term should be elated about higher prices. For the rest of us, rising prices don't really do much for us other than make us feel good for the moment. As a buyer of stocks, we should welcome a down market because it allows us to accumulate more parts of great companies at discount prices.

Straw Hats in the Winter

I usually chuckle when I hear that "investors drove down stock prices today as they took profits." Or "after seeing the unemployment report, investors dumped stocks causing widespread selling." I'm sure you have heard or have seen these headlines after a down day in the stock market. I always wonder, Who are these investors who have a finger on the sell trigger and dump stocks one day just to buy them back the next? And what I really want to know is, what is the media's definition of an investor?

There was a time when investors bought stocks knowing they were buying pieces of a company. An economic report or a few down days couldn't get these investors to dump their shares, or their "babies," as I recall how an old-time client referred to his shares. They were looking for the long term, not 24 to 36 months, but long term as defined by decades.

Imagine how your portfolio would look if you bought or were given shares of Johnson & Johnson (Figure 9.1), Procter & Gamble (Figure 9.2), or Coca Cola (Figure 9.3) more than 35 years ago? I'm sure you would be a very happy camper, as these companies have increased shareholder value over that time period by an enormous amount.

You would have had to hold your shares through the Vietnam War, riots in our cities, civil rights strife, a cold war, resignation of a President, the fall of Saigon, hostages in Iran, inflation, recession . . . well, you get the idea. If you had sold out at every sign of trouble, when would you have bought back in? Instead, the companies that you would've owned continued to march along and grow their business and increase shareholder value.

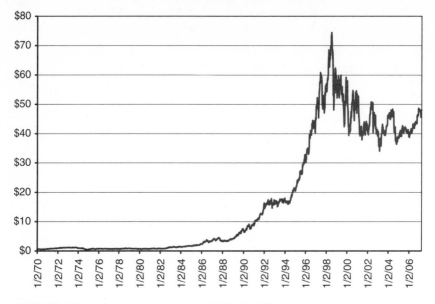

FIGURE 9.1 Johnson & Johnson (1970–2006).

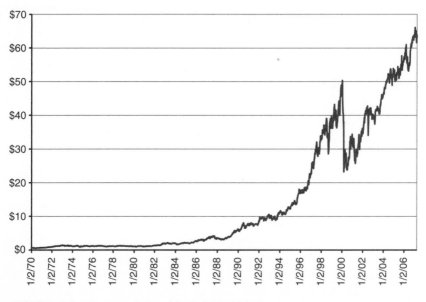

FIGURE 9.2 Procter & Gamble (1970–2006).

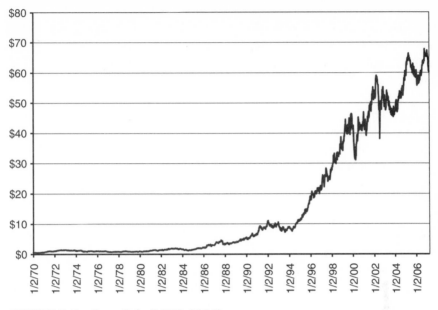

FIGURE 9.3 Coca-Cola (1970–2006).

Due to the tremendous amount of information available instantly, many investors have turned the stock market into a casino, buying when prices are rising and selling when prices are falling. Financier Bernard Baruch remarked more than half a century ago that he had made money in the stock market by buying straw hats in the winter.

Keep in mind that the stock market is not very good at valuing companies. The stock market will sometimes gyrate wildly over a very short span of time for no reason at all. For example, there have been several days in the past five years when the Dow Jones Industrial Average fell more than 1 percent and on the very next day rose by almost the same amount. What changed in our economy in 24 hours that lowered the market capitalization of big multinational companies by billions of dollars one day, only to see them rise the next? As an investor you need to continually remind yourself that small bumps over the short term will yield good results over the long term.

With no apparent news or fundamental change taking place in the company, a long-term investor should welcome prices that bring the valuation of the company lower and should accumulate more shares. Instead of getting depressed, be happy that Mr. Market is bipolar. If you can buy your toothpaste and spaghetti at lower prices, it should bring a smile to your face. Because, over the long term, stock price will eventually reflect the earnings and growth of the company, and that will make for higher share prices and increase the size of your net worth.

It's all a matter of buying companies when they are selling below their underlying value. Lower prices are a good thing when you plan on holding for the long term—it allows you to buy more for less. With these basic but profound points in mind, I implore you to stop focusing on short-term price changes and think about the long term as measured in years, not days. If you are thinking of buying a stock today, in addition to seeking a bargain price, are you willing to hold onto that stock for many months, perhaps even years? Buffett said:

> If you aren't willing to own a stock for ten years, don't even think about owning it for ten minutes. Put together a portfolio of companies whose aggregate earnings march upward over the years, and so also will the portfolio's market value.[3]

Unfortunately his advice gets lost in the daily static of price movements, rumor, and economic reports.

As a long-term investor (translation: *patient* investor), you are going to witness some interesting changes in the companies whose stock you buy. Stock prices will rise and fall, management will come and go, and even the best-managed company will go through periods where sales and earnings are flat. The key is buying the stock at an attractive price. Overpaying for even a great company can produce poor investment returns because it may take a very long time for the economics of the business to catch up with the high price you paid. Paying too high a price is the main reason investors lose patience with their investment and jump ship.

Stock Frustrations

Some time ago, I was having lunch with a good friend who is also a very shrewd investor. He seemed more bothered than usual. After some small talk, he finally opened up. He said, "Charles, I have been investing in the market for years and there is one thing I could never figure out. Why is it that when I buy a stock of a great company, watch its earnings soar, its revenues grow, and all the other things you tell me to consider when investing, the stock price sometimes doesn't budge over the long haul?" I know many other investors who ask themselves the same question.

Here are some real-life examples to shed more light on this frustrating situation. Let's look at a six-year-performance record of two great companies, and see why the stock prices for each didn't increase in relation to the growth of each company. I am sure you'll agree that Wal-Mart and Home Depot are great companies. These two companies are retail giants, in fact combined they had sales of more than $435 billion in 2006. They have wide economic moats, have

TABLE 9.1 Stock Performance over Seven Years			
Company	*12/31/99*	*12/29/06*	*Total Return*
Wal-Mart	$65.17*	$46.18	(29.1%)
Home Depot	$64.85*	$40.16	(38.1%)

*Prices adjusted for splits and dividends
Source: Company filings, public information

been increasing earnings on a yearly basis, and are leaders in their industries. See Table 9.1.

Over the past seven years, had you invested in Wal-Mart or Home Depot, you would have less money at the end of 2006 than you had when you bought the stock at the end of 1999. From this phenomenon, you might assume that earnings fell about the same amount as the stock price. Table 9.2 shows this is not the case—in fact it is quite the opposite.

For most investors, even those who have been investing in the market for years, this seems to be—to quote Winston Churchill—"a riddle wrapped in a mystery inside an enigma." How could companies that, over seven years, increased their earnings by 124.2 percent and 185 percent, respectively, see their stock prices fall rather than rise?

Take Me Out to the—Mania

To begin to find an answer to our question, we need to go back and look at what was happening seven years ago when investors were buying Wal-Mart or Home Depot stock. At the end of 1999 and the beginning of 2000, the stock market was in the grip of a trading mania. I remember taking my kids to see the New York Mets play at Shea Stadium and seeing a large scoreboard that was showing a ticker of the most active shares traded on the NASDAQ that day rather than the box scores of that day's other baseball games.

It seemed that everyone was playing the stock market game, and the media only fueled the mania. They would showcase founders of technology and Internet companies (many of whom were just a few years out of high school) as the new

TABLE 9.2 Earnings per Share (EPS) Growth over Seven Years			
Company	*EPS Yr-End 1999*	*EPS Yr-End 2006*	*5-Yr Total Increase*
Wal-Mart	$1.28	$2.87	124.2%
Home Depot	$1.00	$2.85	185.0%

Source: Company filings, public records

princes and princesses of business. The net worth of some of these whiz kids was often in the hundreds of millions of dollars, and several were valued in the billions. Investors bid stock prices so high that the stock no longer had any relation to the underlying value of the company.

P/E ratio
a stock's market price divided by its current earnings per share. The PE ratio is used by investors as a fundamental measure of the attractiveness of a particular security versus all other securities. The lower the ratio relative to the average of the share market, the lower the market's profit growth expectations.

Many times the stock market becomes irrational because stocks are bought and sold by people who trade with their emotions rather than their brains. When buyers get very greedy or very fearful, they will buy or sell stocks at silly prices. A little more than seven years ago, the stock market was a very greedy place, even more so than usual. Investors pushed stocks to levels that could not be supported by the stocks' underlying true growth. In 2000, when Wal-Mart traded in the high $60 range, investors were willing to pay close to $50 for every $1 of earnings. If written in familiar terms, this is a P/E (price/earnings) ratio of 50. Home Depot, was trading at a *P/E ratio* in the 60s as well. How a company with a market cap in the hundreds of billions could ever be expected to grow earnings at the more than 20 percent a year that would be required to justify such high valuations is beyond me.

I am sure that some of those investors knew that those were ridiculous prices to pay for Wal-Mart and Home Depot. If they sat down with a pencil and paper and figured out the expected earnings growth of those two companies over the next seven years and used a more conservative P/E, they would have realized their folly. But investors were not thinking very clearly then.

What was their justification for paying such lofty prices? It certainly was not that they were buying $1 worth of assets for 50 cents. But at that time, most investors were operating under the greater fool theory of investing, which states that a greater fool will (with any luck) come along and pay a higher price than you did. Investors were considered relics if they were sitting on the sidelines with most of their money in cash rather than stocks. If you didn't own technology stocks, you were missing the boat. Even Warren Buffett was taking heat for his value approach:

> Warren Buffett should say, "I'm sorry," fumed Harry Newton, publisher of *Technology Investor* magazine, in early 2000. How did he miss the silicon, wireless, DSL, cable, and biotech revolutions?[4]

Investors who analyzed a company and came up with a valuation far below the price the stock was trading at that time were told "this time is different." At

TABLE 9.3 Period of Greed						
	2001	2002	2003	2004	2005	2006
EPS	$0.77	$1.00	$1.30	$1.69	$2.20	$2.53
P/E ratio	30	30	30	30	30	15
Stock price		$30				$38

Source: Rothschild, John. *The Davis Dynasty*. New York: John Wiley & Sons, Inc., page 185.

the height of the mania, a well-known columnist and former money manager said:

> We don't use price-to-earnings multiples anymore.... If we talk about price-to-book, we have already gone astray. If we use any of what Graham and Dodd teach us, we wouldn't have a dime under management.[5]

Eventually the bubble burst, and stock prices came back down to more accurately reflect the intrinsic value of their companies. So because many investors had paid very high prices for shares of good companies, they saw their account balances plunge as valuations came in line with historical norms.

Investors take a huge risk when buying stocks if greed is ruling Wall Street. Table 9.3 shows how a stock's performance can actually be hurt when investors give it historically high P/E ratios.

In our example, a company is going gangbusters and is growing earnings at 30 percent over five years. Investors bid the stock up by paying $30 for every $1 of earnings (P/E of 30). Then, in 2006, the company cools off just a bit and sees earnings increase by "only" 15 percent. Wall Street cools to this drop-off in earnings too, and now is willing to pay only a P/E of 15.

The bottom line: Over five years, the stock climbs from $30 a share to $38 a share, for a 6.7 percent annual return. Investors are then left scratching their heads, trying to figure out why the return on the stock was so low, given that earnings zoomed at an annual rate of 20.4 percent during the same period. Perhaps they forgot that they paid a very high multiple (P/E of 30) for growth and were projecting the company would continue to grow earnings at 30 percent.

Price Matters

We all know that everyone has a price. This applies to stocks as well as people. Stocks will, at times, trade at prices that have no relation to the values of the companies. At those times, no matter how much I know about a company's financials, how wide their economic moat, or how fine a job the management is doing, I have to pass on buying the stock and wait for a more sensible price. The Oracle of Omaha, Warren Buffett, reportedly watched Coca-Cola for more than 20 years before he plunged in and bought 7 percent of the company at what he thought was a bargain price in 1988. His $1.3 billion investment is now worth close to $9 billion.

The stock market will bounce around between greed and fear, so don't pay too much attention to daily stock gyrations. When you buy stocks that are trading below their intrinsic value, you are taking out a large chunk of the downside, and time becomes your friend.

The bottom line: The price you pay matters. As I've mentioned earlier, great companies bought at too high a price can produce terrible results. But I have shown you only one example so far, based on the study of a period of apathy. Applying the same side-by-side analysis to two different companies, and noting the important difference between "price" and "value," you improve your insight even more.

A Tale of Two Companies

Many investors place too much emphasis on the price of a stock and not on the value they are getting. These same investors would never buy a $50 stock because they view it as "too expensive." They would much rather stick with buying stocks that are trading for $20 or less thinking they are cheap. I never could understand their logic because I view expensive and cheap as relative terms.

Assume you were in the market for a new car and set a budget for buying one at no more than $30,000. You went to a Lexus dealer and fell in love with the 2007 IS sports luxury sedan, which retails for about $30,000. Things couldn't be better; you found the car of your dreams at the amount you had budgeted. But let's assume right before you told the salesperson to "wrap it up," you were offered the top of the line LS luxury sedan, which normally retails for about $65,000 for $40,000 because it was used as a demo. Would you buy it? If you didn't have the extra $10,000, you really had no choice and would have had to decline the offer. But what if you could afford the extra expense? Would you buy the luxury model at a steep discount or stick to your budget and buy the $30,000 model?

If you look at the example based on price alone, you are making a decision based on either spending $30,000 or $40,000. Price is the underlying factor in your decision regardless of what value you are receiving in return. On the other hand if you view the example based on value, in one case you are spending $30,000 to get $30,000 of value and in the other case you are spending $40,000 to get $65,000 in value. If you make a decision based on price alone, you will miss out on a great bargain.

TABLE 9.4 Circuit City versus MSC Industrial Direct		
	Circuit City	*MSC Industrial Direct*
Stock Price	$20	$45
5-Year Annual Sales Growth	−2.5%	10%
5-Year Annual Earnings per Share Growth	−26.0%	33%
Return on Equity (2006)	10.0%	21.3%
Net Profit Margin (2006)	1.5%	10.3%
Market Cap	$3.5 billion	$3.0 billion

Now let's apply this to investing. MSC Industrial Direct is trading at $44 per share and Circuit City is trading at $20 per share (as of March 2007). Which one is cheaper stock? Based on price alone it would appear that Circuit City at $20 per share is cheaper. As we discussed earlier, a stock is really a part ownership of a business and should be viewed in that light. Look at a few key fundamentals of each company and ask yourself which company would you rather buy a piece of? See Table 9.4.

Although Circuit City is selling at a lower stock price, you are buying a piece of a business that over the past five years has not been able to increase sales or earnings, works on a razor-thin margin, and has a fair return on equity. While MSC Industrial's stock price is more than double that of Circuit City, you are buying company that has seen sales and earnings soar, works on a healthy net profit margin, and has been able to return a high rate on equity.

When looking for investment opportunities, don't handicap yourself by focusing on price. Your goal should not be to pay the lowest price but instead to get the best value. In the next section I show you how to determine a fair price to pay for a great company. If you know simple math skills like division and multiplication, you should have no problem figuring this out. It's not complicated any more than it is to find a company with superior performance.

Don't worry so much about the math; just keep in mind that you are trying to value a business. As Buffett said:

> If calculus were required, I'd have to go back to delivering papers. I've never seen any need for algebra. Essentially, you're trying to figure out the value of a business. It's true that you have to divide by the number of shares outstanding, so division is required. If you were going out to buy a farm or an apartment house or a dry cleaning establishment, I really don't think you'd have to take someone along to do calculus. Whether you made the right purchase or not would depend on the future earning ability of that enterprise, and then relating that to the price you are being asked for the asset.[6]

How to Determine a Fair Price

My wife and I took our family on a well-deserved vacation. New York winters can be brutal at times, so each January we search out a warm destination for some fun in the sun. One year we split our vacation time between Disney World and the beaches of Miami in sunny Florida. While most people are lying on their lounges reading a mystery or trashy romance novel, my reading material is a little out of the norm. I usually travel with ten to fifteen company annual reports. To be quite honest with you, I really enjoy learning about companies and different industries. For me reading annual reports is relaxing.

One bright sunny morning I got down to the pool early to catch up on my reading. However, this morning my quiet time was interrupted. Seeing that I had a stack of annual reports on the table next to me, a middle-aged man a few lounges over struck up a conversation with me about investing. After a few minutes of chitchat he confided to me that when it came to his investing, he found it easy to pick the right company but hard to know what price to pay. He started sharing his stories on how, more times than he cared to recall, he would buy a stock, watch the company's financials soar—yet the stock would go sideways or down. I shared with him that his problem is not at all uncommon among investors. Most investors have no idea how to determine the price to pay for a share of stock.

It's quite obvious that choosing companies that are performing well is extremely important. You need to find companies that are growing their earnings, have high return on equity, and have enduring competitive advantages. As we saw with the examples of Wal-Mart and Home Depot, great companies can make lousy investments if purchased at the wrong price. Very few investors take the time to figure out what price to pay for the stock. A great company purchased at a high price will produce terrible returns, while that same company purchased at an attractive price will produce excellent returns. I want to share with you how I go about determining whether a company's stock is attractively priced.

Charlie Munger's Three Great Lessons of Investing[7]

1. "A great business at a fair price is superior to a fair business at a great price."
2. "A great business at a fair price is superior to a fair business at a great price."
3. "A great business at a fair price is superior to a fair business at a great price."

Looking Backward: Graham and Dodd

Before we attempt to determine a fair price to pay for a stock, we need to look back at three main characteristics defined by Graham and Dodd over 70 years ago:

1. Stock prices can have extreme short term price volatility (aka Mr. Market).

2. Yet, the underlying company's financial statements are relatively stable.

3. So, a strategy of buying stocks when prices are significantly below the calculated intrinsic value of the company will produce superior results (aka buying with a margin of safety).[8]

Professor Bruce C.N. Greenwald of Columbia Business School stated that value investing is relatively simple:

> A value investor estimates the fundamental value of a financial security and compares that value to the current price Mr. Market is offering. If price is lower than value by a sufficient margin of safety, the value investor buys the security.[9]

How then does one figure out the "calculated intrinsic value of a company" so they can buy the stock below that value? There are basically three approaches one can take toward valuing a company.

1. *Stock selling below reproduction cost of its current assets.*[10] This approach requires one to go through the balance sheet of a company with a fine-toothed comb. Many times what is acceptable for Generally Accepted Accounting Principles (GAAP) does not truly reflect the value of the asset. In addition, sometimes a company's stock will trade for a lower price than the book value of the company. Ben Graham focused on this approach toward valuing a company.

    The main drawback is that it requires fluency in accounting and specialized knowledge so that you can properly value the assets and liabilities.

2. *Private transaction and formula valuation.* This approach establishes the price of the company based on what a company would realize if the sale was negotiated by a rationally motivated buyer and seller. For example, most money management firms are bought and sold based on a percentage of money under management. If money management

company ABC has $10 billion under management, the going price would be established as 2 percent of assets under management, or $200 million. If ABC is trading at a stock price that values the company at $175 million, an investor taking the private transaction approach would say that ABC is undervalued.

Private transaction valuation requires one to keep up with similar transactions in an industry and to be able to make modifications to the valuation. All companies are not exactly alike and therefore all valuations will be different. Also during times of market exuberance when sales are being transacted at highly inflated prices, private transaction sales could overvalue public companies and not be a good arbiter of value. This approach is best left in the hands of experts who specialize in certain industries and can accurately determine value due to access of private transactions that take place in that industry.

3. *Valuations based on future earnings.* This approach requires one to make an assumption about future earnings growth and be willing to pay a high multiple for those earnings. For example, assume Google's earnings per share are $10 and the stock is trading at $400 per share, a P/E of 40. An investor valuing Google based on future earnings growth could make the case that Google is really cheap. The assumption could be that mediocre advertising firms trade at P/Es of 25 and that given Google's growth, in two years' time earnings should grow at 50 percent per year and be at $22.50. Applying the advertising industry average P/E of 25 would give Google a price of ($22.50 projected EPS × P/E of 25) = $563 per share, or 40 percent higher than its current price.

The problem with this approach is that one needs to price in a very cheery future. It leaves no room for error as a high P/E and continued above average earnings growth are assumed. This approach was one of the main drives for extreme valuations of technology and Internet companies during the dot.com bubble, however the future is uncertain and trees don't grow to the sky. In addition, P/E is not a fair valuation method, but a reflection of the market's expectation of future value. History has shown that high P/E stocks under-perform the averages, meaning that the typical projected P/E tends to be too optimistic.[11]

A Simple Approach to Valuation

In 1938 John Burr Williams published a book based on his Ph.D. thesis called *The Theory of Investment Value*. He provided a way to come up with an intrinsic value of any security. In a nutshell Williams wrote that the worth of a business is found by estimating all the cash a company will earn over its lifetime and then discount it back to present-day dollars.

Buffett uses a similar approach and defines intrinsic value as the "discounted value of the cash that can be taken out of a business during its remaining life."[12] When comparing the value of businesses he said that this approach is "the only logical way to evaluate the relative attractiveness of investments and businesses."[13]

In other words, the way to value a business is to research the stream of earnings a company has produced over the past several years and then try to project what it will generate over the next five or so years. Of course, the main pitfall with any projection is that the future is uncertain. How then can we accurately project future earnings if we don't have a crystal ball? Is there a way to increase our chances of predicting earnings growth over the next five years?

Fortunately the answer is that it is possible. By following this approach, we can eliminate many of the companies that will never have a snowball's chance in hell of ever making money and can avoid the glamor stocks that merely serve as lottery tickets for the uninitiated investor.

The Stock Universe

Williams and Buffett have told us that in order to find a company's intrinsic value, we need to estimate the earnings stream the company will be able to produce going forward. Buffett gives us some insight into the types of companies he focuses on to begin his analysis:

> Your goal as an investor should simply be to purchase, at a rational price, a part interest in an easily understandable business whose earnings are virtually certain to be materially higher 5, 10, and 20 years from now.[14]

Buffett is telling us to purchase companies whose earnings are predictable and consistent. While nothing is guaranteed, certain companies have a much higher probability of producing higher earnings over the foreseeable future. Our first step should then be to select companies that have demonstrated the ability to produce consistent and predictable earnings in the past and are in industries that are easily understandable.

Using the Value Line Investment Survey universe of 1,700 stocks, we screen for companies that have been able to grow their earnings at an annualized rate of 10 percent over the past 10 years. This screen narrows our list to 451 companies. Our next screen is to find companies that have a Value Line earnings predictability rating of 75 or greater (a ranking based on 0 = predictable to

100 = very predictable). Our universe shrinks to 218 companies. By applying two very simple screens, we have eliminated close to 1,500 companies that have not been able to grow earnings per share at an annualized rate of 10 percent over the past 10 years and/or have not done so predictably and consistently.

Companies that are able to grow their earnings in a consistent and predictable pattern for an extended period of time are often great businesses led by good management. One more screen that we can use to make our universe even smaller is to focus on companies that have been able to produce an ROE greater than 15 percent. This screen will separate the great from the good companies since a company with an ROE of 15 percent or greater is truly "best of breed." Applying this screen, we are now left with 152 companies.

By focusing on companies with consistent and predictable operating histories and that have high ROEs, we can now have added confidence in predicting earnings growth over the next five years. See Table 9.5.

A Simple Approach

dividend payout ratio
The percentage of earnings paid in cash to shareholders. It is calculated by dividing the dividends paid by the earnings per share (Example: dividend of .52 / EPS $1.36 = 38%).

Once you have defined your universe, the next step we need to do is separate what we know and what we don't know so we can establish the price we want to pay.

Here is the information we do know about the company as we work our way to trying to determine the price we want to pay to get an adequate return on our investment. We will use International Gaming Technologies (NYSE: IGT), a leading manufacturer of slot machines and related software for our example.

Company Ticker IGT	International Gaming Technologies
Price	44.02
EPS (ttm)	$1.36
P/E	32
Dividend	$.52
Dividend payout ratio	38%
EPS-Growth 10-year	19%
Value Line earnings predictability	75

1. The first step we need to take in order to determine the price we want to pay for the stock is to project EPS growth over the next five years and project a P/E.

TABLE 9.5 Some of the Companies That Make the Screen

Company	Ticker	EPS/Predictability	ROE	EPS Growth 10-Year
Colgate-Palmolive	CL	100	109%	11%
Hershey Co.	HSY	100	56%	10%
SLM Corporation	SLM	100	36%	17%
Microsoft Corp.	MSFT	100	31%	22%
Wiley (John) & Sons	JW-A	100	31%	18%
Medtronic, Inc.	MDT	100	29%	19%
Johnson & Johnson	JNJ	100	28%	15%
McGraw-Hill	MHP	100	26%	15%
Starbucks Corp.	SBUX	100	26%	30%
Bed Bath & Beyond	BBBY	100	25%	31%
Wrigley (Wm.) Jr.	WWY	100	25%	10%
Donaldson Co.	DCI	100	24%	14%
Biomet	BMET	100	24%	17%
Stryker Corp.	SYK	100	22%	23%
Bard (C.R.)	BCR	100	21%	11%
Praxair Inc.	PX	100	21%	12%
Wal-Mart Stores	WMT	100	21%	16%
Bank of Nova Scotia	BNS.TO	100	21%	14%
Omnicom Group	OMC	100	20%	17%
Sonic Corp.	SONC	100	20%	21%
Total System Svcs.	TSS	100	19%	21%
First Midwest Bancorp	FMBI	100	19%	10%
ITT Corp.	ITT	100	18%	15%
Fiserv Inc.	FISV	100	18%	22%
Church & Dwight	CHD	100	18%	18%
Synovus Financial	SNV	100	18%	14%
Dentsply Int'l	XRAY	100	17%	14%
Walgreen Co.	WAG	100	17%	17%
Commerce Bancshs.	CBSH	100	17%	11%
Matthews Int'l	MATW	100	17%	15%
Aflac Inc.	AFL	100	16%	17%
City National Corp.	CYN	100	16%	24%
Patterson Cos.	PDCO	100	16%	22%
Cintas Corp.	CTAS	100	16%	15%
Marshall & Ilsley	MI	100	16%	13%

Source: Value Line Investment Summary 2–19-07

In order to project EPS growth over the next five years, we will use a simple formula using only two variables.

- If the company's EPS-growth was greater than 15 percent over the past 10 years, use 15 percent as the projection.
- If the company's EPS-growth was lower than 15 percent over the past 10 years, use 10 percent as the projection.

Since we want to have a margin of safety and assume the future will never be as good as we might think, we want to use an EPS growth rate that is conservative yet takes into consideration a company's past performance. Very few companies are able to achieve EPS growth rates above 15 percent for long periods of time.[15] Therefore that will be the highest EPS we will use for our projections.

IGT's 10-year EPS growth rate was 19 percent, so we use 15 percent for our 5-year EPS growth projection.

2. To project a P/E at the end of five years, once again we use a simple approach.

- If the company's current P/E is above 20, then use a P/E of 17.
- If the company's current P/E is 20 or lower, then use a P/E of 12.

Historically the stock market has averaged a P/E of 17 over the past 50 years. Very few companies have been able to trade at a P/E of 17 or higher for long periods of time. If the company's P/E is less than 20, we use a margin of safety and project a modest P/E of 12.

Since IGT's current P/E is 32 we use a projected P/E of 17.

We now have the two numbers we need to begin the process of determining the price we want to pay. To review, we are using a projected EPS 5-year growth rate of 15 percet and a P/E of 17 to determine the price we want to pay for IGT today.

Step 1: Earnings per Share in Five Years Based on 15 Percent Growth

We begin by compounding the current EPS (TTM) of $1.36 by 15 percent per year for the next five years.

Multiply the current EPS ($1.36) by 1.15 to get end-of-year EPS. (See Table 9.6).

Step 2: Multiply Projected PE by Projected EPS at End Year 5

We now know that if IGT can grow their EPS by 15 percent per annum over the next 5 years, the EPS at the end of the fifth year would be $2.73.

TABLE 9.6 Projected EPS		
	15% Projection	*Projected EPS at Year End*
End Year 1	$1.36 × 1.15	$1.56
End Year 2	$1.56 × 1.15	$1.80
End Year 3	$1.80 × 1.15	$2.07
End Year 4	$2.07 × 1.15	$2.38
End Year 5	$2.38 × 1.15	$2.73

The P/E we are using is 17. By multiplying the projected EPS at the end of the fifth year ($2.73) by our projected P/E (17), IGT's stock price will be trading at $46.41.

Step 3: Calculate Earnings Paid Out As Dividends

Along the way IGT paid out part of its earnings as cash or commonly referred to as dividends. The dividend payout ratio tells us that 38 percent of earnings are currently paid as dividends. Adding up all the earnings we will have over the 5 year period comes out to $10.54 ($1.56 + $1.80 + $2.07 + $2.38 + $2.73 = $10.54). By multiplying the total EPS earned over the 5 years ($10.54) by the dividend payout ratio of 38 percent, we project that $4.00 will be paid out to us in dividends ($10.54 × 38% = $4.00).

Step 4: Getting the Total Share Price

By adding IGT's stock price at the end of Year 5 ($46.41) to the dividends paid out over the same time of $4.00, we get a total stock price at the end of Year 5 of $50.41 ($46.41 + $4.00).

We have just figured out that if IGT can grow the EPS over the next 5 years by 15 percent and trade at a P/E of 17, the future stock price will be $50.41.

The next step we need to figure out is what price we would need to pay today so that we can achieve a good return on our investment. For that we need to set a benchmark of what type of return we want on our money over the next five years.

If we would put the money that we earmarked for IGT into a conservative and safe investment, like a 5-year Treasury note, we could make about 4.6 percent per year on our investment. We would definitely want to make more than that since anybody with a pulse can buy the Treasury note and with no effort or risk make a guaranteed 4.6 percent return. If we are going to invest in a stock, we would want to be compensated for taking on additional risk above and beyond what we can make in a Treasury note. This is known as the equity risk premium. This is the additional return that the stock market needs to provide us over the risk free rate (of the 4.6% Treasury note).

Historically investors have used 6 percent as the equity risk premium, so in our example we would need our investment in IGT to return at least 10.6 percent per annum over the next five years (4.6% + 6%). We can also use a higher hurdle such as the one Buffett uses. "Before Buffett buys shares of a company, he makes sure the stock is capable of returning at least 15 percent a year for him over a long period."[16]

A 15 percent return is possible if we purchase the right company and, just as importantly, pay the right price.

Step 5: Price to Pay to Achieve Required Return

Based on our assumptions for IGT, we figured out that it would be trading at $50.41 at the end of 5 years. What price would we need to pay today to achieve a 15 percent return?

To find out the highest price you should be willing to pay to achieve a 15 percent return is to divide the price of IGT at the end of the fifth year ($50.41) by 1.15 for each of 5 years. See Table 9.7.

The highest price to pay today to achieve a 15 percent return would be $25.06. Currently IGT is trading at $40 per share, so we would need to wait until the price comes down before making a purchase. Please note that you should use a range in order to determine the price to pay. Since we are trying to value a multi-billion company, don't get fixated on the $25.06 price. If the stock trades in the $25 to $26 area, it still would constitute a good purchase.

If you would prefer a lower required rate of return like 12 percent, all you would need to do is divide the price of IGT at the end of the fifth year ($50.41) by 1.12. If you required a 10 percent return, then divide by 1.10. See Table 9.8.

TABLE 9.7 Price Calculation		
	EPS, 15% Hurdle Rate	*Present Price to Pay for Stock*
Year 5	$50.41 ÷ 1.15	$43.83
Year 4	$43.83 ÷ 1.15	$38.12
Year 3	$38.12 ÷ 1.15	$33.14
Year 2	$33.14 ÷ 1.15	$28.82
Year 1	$28.82 ÷ 1.15	$25.06

TABLE 9.8 Highest Price to Pay for Required Return	
Return Desired	Highest Price to Pay
15%	$25.06
12%	$28.60
10%	$31.30

Please note that if you are willing to pay a higher stock price, you will get a lower return. If you bought IGT at $25 per share and I bought it for $31 per share, at the end of five years (assuming our projections came to pass), you would end up with a 15 percent annualized return and I would end up with a 10 percent annualized return. That is why value investors have great patience and will make a purchase only when they can achieve the required rate of return on their investment. What happens if after doing all your analysis the price of the stock is not near the price you are willing to pay to earn a certain rate of return? You wait. Patience is a very important key to investing. Investing smartly is buying only at your price, unlike the average investor who falls in love with a company and buys at any price. If you buy stocks with a margin of safety and don't overpay, you will see your account continue to grow year after year.

> *Never count on making a good sale. Have the purchase price be so attractive that even a mediocre sale gives good results.*[17]
> —*Warren Buffett*

Why Stocks Trade at a Discount

Why do stocks sometimes sell at a big discount to their underlying value? I'm sure some of what I have to say will be an eye-opener. So sit back, grab yourself another cup of tea, and let me enlighten you as to why the stock market gyrates like a whirling dervish.

At the end of each day the New York Stock Exchange (NYSE) lists how much volume was traded on the exchange. I remember it like it was yesterday when I first heard over the radio in 1982 that the NYSE traded 100 million shares for the first time. What was big news then is now just a drop in the bucket. Today if the NYSE trades less than *one billion shares*, it's considered a slow day. What is the reason for all this volume? Are investors that fickle that they trade more than one billion shares a day with each other?

To find the reason we need to look back to 1950. Back then only 9 percent of financial institutions owned stocks. Few institutions owned stocks especially since the worst depression in this country's history was still fresh in their minds. However today the picture is completely different. Currently more than 68 percent of financial institutions own stocks. You might think that with so many professional and sophisticated investors owning stocks, trading volume should be going down, not up. Professionals surely would know the benefits of buying good companies and holding them for the long term. Sad to say that is not the case. Between 1990 and 2005, the average equity mutual funds turned over their portfolio 91 percent per year. In other words, if you looked at their portfolio on January 1, and again on December 31, 91 percent of the stocks in their portfolio would have changed. Contrast that with a 17 percent turnover per year (a little more than once every 5 years) that equity mutual funds had between 1950 and 1965. In the good old days investors used to hold stocks for the long run.[18]

Once upon a time stocks were bought and many times passed from generation to generation as investors saw the value of owning great companies forever. What happened to thinking of stocks as pieces of companies? Why are these supposed sophisticated investors turning over their stocks at such a rapid pace? And more importantly how does that give the sane, rational thinking investor an edge?

It's the Structure

You have to feel bad for many of these financial institutions because the system works against them forcing them to make foolish decisions. Today performance is measured in weeks instead of decades. Institutions are under tremendous pressure to play the performance game. Not only do they have to put up good numbers over short periods of time, they also have to have good "relative performance," which means how well they performed against an index and their peers.

A fund that produced a 10 percent return in a quarter does not look very good if the index they are measured against returned 12 percent. The fund will be labeled an "underperformer" and the manager will start taking a lot of heat. At this point it becomes extremely difficult for the manager to buy stocks that do not track the index for fear of drifting too far from it. There is no way that the manager will fight the crowd and buy stocks that are not very popular at the moment. Like other lemmings jumping off the cliff, the manager now gets caught into buying and selling the same popular themes and ideas as everyone else. And that is just one way great companies selling at discounted prices get overlooked on Wall Street.

Opportunity for the Rest of Us

Another way great companies sell at discounted prices has more to do with computer algorithms than fundamentals. A trading strategy employed by professionals that creates enormous volume and large volatility is called program trading. For the last week of 2006, program trading amounted to 34 percent of NYSE average daily volume of 1.9 million shares, or 676 million program shares traded per day.[19] It never ceases to amaze me that more than one-third of the shares traded on a daily basis on the NYSE changed hands for no fundamental reason regarding the company!

> *We believe that according the name "investor" to institutions that*
> *trade actively is like calling someone who repeatedly*
> *engages in one–night stands a romantic.*[20]
> *—Warren Buffett*

Another cause of wild swings is the addition or deletion of a company from a major index. If a stock is added to the S&P 500 index and at the same time a stock that had been part of the index is taken out, index funds will need to sell the stock that is leaving the index and buy the stock that is being added to the index. In November 2005 the S&P 500 reconfigured the way it calculates its index and Wal-Mart among other companies would then have less of an impact on the index. Index fund managers needed to lower their exposure to Wal-Mart in order to track the S&P 500 index. Over the course of several days, hundreds of millions of dollars were shaved off Wal-Mart's market cap for no fundamental reason other than index funds needed to realign their portfolios.

Program trading trades where 15 or more stocks are traded in order to capture small price discrepancies among stocks, options, and futures.

These are just two types of temporary price shocks which are music to a value investor's ears. That is why the stock market is a terrible arbiter of value because more often than not it is valuing companies based on everything but their underlying value. Once you determine the price you want to pay for the stock, wait for Mr. Market to come to your price. Sometimes Mr. Market gives me my price and other times he doesn't. Your goal is to buy only on your terms and at your price.

It sometimes takes courage to buy when everyone else is selling. Over the long term buying good companies at good prices and especially those with no debt has made more rich investors than any other strategy I know. Eventually the stock price converges with the intrinsic value of the company. The way the stock market falls and rises, often without any reason at all, creates a great opportunity for the investor with patience.

Chairman (Sen. William Fulbright): One other question and I will desist. What causes a cheap stock to find its value?
Benjamin Graham: That is one of the mysteries of our business and it is a mystery to me as well as to everybody else. [But] we know from experience that eventually the market catches up with value.
—*Testimony to the Committee on Banking and Commerce, March 11, 1955*

That is really the key. An old adage reminds us that "the market rewards patience." Accompany this with a little contrarian focus on what really matters and you will be able to avoid the temptation coming from your own worst enemy. I explain exactly what I mean by this in the next chapter.

Key Points

1. The stock market does not do a good job at valuing companies, but it is a great reflection of greed and fear. Short-term price gyrations are symptoms of this behavior, but long-term investors are well-advised to ignore today's erratic price movement and establish a very long-term price horizon.

2. Those who follow the current fad might make short-term speculative profits. But the greater fool approach to investing eventually fails. You don't want to wake up one morning to discover that the greater fool staring back at you from the mirror—is you!

3. The price you pay for a stock will have the greatest influence on your return. Great companies bought at lousy prices produce terrible returns.

10
Chapter

Your Own Worst Enemy

If you formed a conclusion from the facts and if you know your judgment is sound, act on it—even though others may hesitate or differ. You're neither right nor wrong because the crowd disagrees with you. You are right because your data and reasoning are right.[1]

—Benjamin Graham

My favorite season of the year? Spring. Living in New York, where the winters can sometimes be brutal, there is nothing like the smell of spring in the city. Besides being able to walk outside without a heavy coat and gloves, spring is also the start of the baseball season. I literally count down the days until the start of the baseball season and try to go to as many games as I can over the next six months.

Lessons learned in baseball can make you a better investor. Ted Williams, one of the greatest hitters of all time, used the discipline of waiting for the right pitch. Williams would swing only at balls that would give him a very high percentage of hits, and he avoided balls that would reduce those chances. Warren Buffett says he follows the same discipline as Williams: "Swing" at businesses that have attractive prices and high returns, and let the fully priced businesses pass by.

Most investors do the exact opposite—they swing at every pitch. They also tend to focus on the short term and disregard the big picture. Recently there was an article in the *Wall Street Journal*[2] that talked about the disappointing results of several top mutual fund managers. Despite their great long-term track records, they posted "lousy returns last year." My first reaction was, "So what?" What difference does one year make? Is a manager supposed to have a great year every year?

Bill Miller, manager of Legg Mason's Value Trust Fund, the only manager to beat the S&P 500 index each year for 15 calendar years in a row, wrote the year before his streak ended:

> If your expectation is that we will outperform the market every year, you can expect to be disappointed. We would love nothing better than to beat the market every day, every month, every quarter and every year. Unfortunately, when we purchase companies we believe are mispriced, it is often difficult to determine when the market will agree with us and close the discount to intrinsic value. Our goal is to construct portfolios that have the potential to outperform the market over an investment time horizon of 3–5 years without assuming undue risk. If we achieve that goal, we believe we will be doing our job, whether we beat the market each and every year or not.[3]

If Bill Miller is saying that his first goal is to build a portfolio that has the potential to outperform the market over a long time frame, why are so many investors fixated on a much shorter time frame? I think part of the blame for this shortsighted thinking has to do with the media, and another part has to do with information overload.

There are several cable channels that run stock prices at the bottom of the screen from market open to close and beyond. You can now watch every wiggle of a stock's movement and observe your fortunes rise and fall with each trade. Economic announcements (more than 300 of them a year!) are made into headline news and, in turn, stock prices sometimes gyrate wildly before after these announcements are made. Investors are led to believe that all this information is important, and that it has a direct impact on a company's long-term performance. Nothing could be further from the truth. Over a five-year period, the price of a stock will greatly track the fundamentals of the company and not quarterly economic reports. We live in a world in which information on virtually anything is no further than the Internet. With the ability to access information and the media reporting on the stock market as if it were a sports event, investors lose track of the long term and focus too much on the short term.

Periods of Disappointment

Other than Bill Miller of Legg Mason and his amazing 15-year record of beating the S&P 500 each and every year, every great investor had times when they underperformed the S&P 500 index over short periods of time. In Robert

Hagstrom's excellent book *The Warren Buffett Portfolio: Mastering the Strategy of the Focus Investment Strategy*, he shows the record of managers who had excellent long-term performance, but had periods of disappointment over the short term. The investors he talks about besides Buffett are John Maynard Keynes (British economist), Charles Munger (vice chairman of Berkshire Hathaway), Bill Ruane (Sequoia Fund) and Lou Simpson (co-chairman of GEICO Insurance). On average, this superstar lineup of managers underperformed the S&P 500 index close to 33% of the time. In fact, on average, the number of consecutive years they underperformed the S&P 500 was 2.75 years.

Profile: Bill Ruane

In 1969 when Warren Buffett closed his partnership, many of the partners wanted to know whom to invest with. Buffett recommended Bill Ruane, a fellow classmate he had met when they both were taking Ben Graham's course on security analysis at Columbia University in 1951.

Ruane's investment strategy was to buy good businesses that could raise the price of their products or service without seeing a dropoff in revenue or earnings. He also required that the business have low capital requirements and generate a large portion of their earnings in cash. Ruane would make a purchase only when the stock was selling significantly below the underlying worth of the business, which he determined as the price that would be negotiated by rationally motivated principles. Return on capital, in Ruane's approach, was the most important input. The Sequoia Fund has a compounded annualized return of 15.7 percent (1970–2006), versus 11.8 percent for the S&P 500.

If these managers had started their careers during the dot-com mania (between 1998 and 2000), odds are they would have had a very hard time raising assets or staying employed as mutual fund managers. Great companies with solid earnings were falling in price as tech and Internet companies were soaring, which made value investors look foolish. Yet each one of these investors had outstanding returns over the long term. All of these managers outperformed the S&P 500 yet suffered a few "lousy years" (Table 10.1).

Back to Baseball

Many times, the way we view events in the world of investing is radically different from the way we view them in the real world. An example that will highlight this

TABLE 10.1 Long-Term Performance of Superstar Managers

Manager	Number of Years	Average Return	S&P 500 Return	Annual Outperformance of S&P 500
John Maynard Keynes	18	13.2%	−0.1%	13.2%
Charles Munger	14	24.3%	6.4%	17.9%
Bill Ruane	36	15.9%	11.8%	4.1%
Lou Simpson	17	24.7%	17.8%	6.9%

Source: Robert G. Hagstrom, *The Warren Buffett Portfolio*, John Wiley & Sons, 1999.

point can be found in baseball. In 2005 Chicago Cubs first baseman Derek Lee led the National League in batting average. He finished the year with a batting average of .335, an extraordinary average. Yet if we look at Lee's results on a shorter time frame, the way many investors judge their returns on stocks, during some months he was not all-star material. For example, in the month of August, Lee batted only .284. While still a high average, it might have disappointed some, especially after he had batted .407 in June and .303 in July. You could have drawn the conclusion that Lee should be traded, since he might have lost his touch. As silly as that sounds, many investors look at investing in the same light. The longer the time frame, the more the cream will rise to the top and great companies will produce excellent returns.

Don't Open Your Mail

The best advice I can give you is to stay focused on why you invested in a stock. If you are not prepared to hold it for five or more years, you shouldn't buy it. Short-term gyrations in the market are there to help you, since they allow you to buy great companies at even better prices. Don't let the short term knock you out of a position. Do your research, invest in a great company selling at an attractive price and then, when you get your monthly brokerage statement, don't open your mail. Let the company's fundamentals tell you the real story of where the stock will go over the long term. Have the patience to stick with a good company when the waters are choppy. Don't let Mr. Market separate you from a great company simply because the price went down. The biggest factor holding many investors back from achieving great results is not the company, the stock market, or the media—it is they themselves. Marc Antony could just as easily have been giving Brutus advice on investing when he said, "The fault, dear Brutus, is not in our stars, but in ourselves."[4]

Stay the Course

If you ask the average person what it takes to be a successful investor, I am sure these two traits would be the first things that pop into most people's minds: hard work and intelligence. We live in a very competitive society, and most of us equate hard work with success. Most people have an image of a successful investor as someone who wakes up at the crack of dawn to check the overseas markets, has a desk full of computer screens watching every wiggle the market makes, and wears a headset while barking orders to his brokers. In addition, the successful investor must be real smart—writing formulas in complex spreadsheets as he tries to discern the market's next big move.

I, too, used to have that image in my mind of a successful investor. However, over the past several years that image has changed. I have read about and have met many successful value investors, and they are a far cry from the image most people have in their heads. Sure, hard work and intelligence are very important to becoming a success; however, there are several other traits that one needs to possess as well. I have found that there are three main traits that successful value investors all have in common. Before I share them with you, I want to point out the most important thing they all start off with—the discipline to stay the course no matter how bad things look over the short term.

Looking Dumb

I don't think any value manager was more out of favor than Don Yacktman, portfolio manager of the Yacktman Fund, in 1999. Don was named Morningstar Inc.'s Portfolio Manager of the Year in 1991, but a few years later, in 1999, his fund was one of the worst performers in its category, falling close to 17 percent while the S&P was up 19.5 percent, (a difference of more than 36%!). His board of directors disagreed with his value strategy so strongly that new directors were installed in the fourth quarter of 1998.

Don is a very disciplined man. Even though he saw assets in his funds plummet, was mocked in the media for holding onto stocks that kept going lower; he did not stray from a philosophy of buying stocks trading at a discount to their underlying value. His discipline was rewarded as the dot-com bubble burst and the stocks in his portfolio began to soar. In fact all of the fund's 10-year rolling performance has exceeded the S&P 500 index. As Don's discipline has shown, value investors are truly a breed apart.

I don't think this happened because value investors work harder or are more intelligent than most. I think it is because they think differently from the crowd. Let me share with you the three traits all have in common and how you, too, can have superior returns if you develop their traits.

1. *The way they think separates them from the crowd.* I went back to 1999 and selected four mutual funds that all have excellent managers. All the funds I chose had different investment styles and very few owned the same stocks. The two things all had in common were an experienced manager and a philosophy of buying undervalued and out-of-favor stocks. I chose 1999 because that was the height of the stock market bubble. That year the NASDAQ soared close to 89 percent, and valuations, we were told, didn't matter in this new paradigm.

   These four funds all underperformed the S&P 500, and several of them saw their portfolio values decline. The pressure to abandon a philosophy that had worked for so long was enormous. Yet these four managers did not waver. They did not buy stocks that were touted in the media, nor did they buy the hype that earnings didn't matter anymore. They separated from the crowd and continued to buy stocks of companies that were selling for less than their underlying value.

   On average, these four funds underperformed the S&P 500 by more than 21 percent. Over the short term their managers continued to stick to their guns and stand out from the crowd even more. However, over the past five years, they had the last laugh as their performance outperformed the S&P 500[5] by a wide margin. See Figures 10.1 and 10.2.

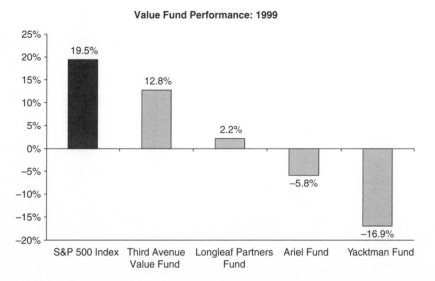

FIGURE 10.1 1999: Disappointing One Year Performance.

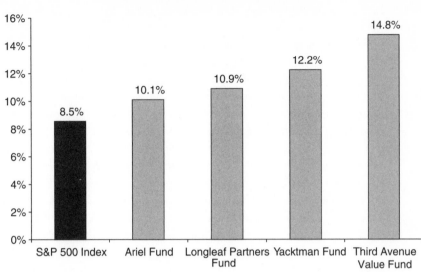

FIGURE 10.2 All Funds 5-Year Average Return Outperformed the S&P 500.
Period: 5 years ending May 18, 2007.

Those same funds that had underperformed the S&P 500 so badly in 1999 outperformed the S&P 500 by an average of 3.45 percent per year over the past five years. The funds' under-performance in 1999 and the five-year performance *were all achieved by the same managers*. The ability to separate from the crowd is what makes these managers stand out.

2. *They challenge the conventional wisdom.* Very few people are bold and confident enough to stand out from the crowd. The old saying that the nail that sticks out gets hammered down has become the mantra at many corporations and money management firms. I remember that when personal computer sales started to rise more than 25 years ago, purchasing managers continued to buy IBM PCs even though PC clones were selling at much lower prices. Purchasing managers justified this by saying that "nobody got fired for buying IBM."

Value investors are constantly challenging the conventional wisdom (CW) because that is where the value is. Most investors feel more secure buying what in the past delivered consistent and rising performance. The problem is they overpay, which over time leads to poor performance. Investors didn't care what price they paid for Yahoo, Cisco, or Sun Microsystems at the height of the tech mania in 2000.

The CW said that these companies would continue to grow and what seemed like a high price would be a cheap price five years later. Because investors did not question the CW, they went along for the ride and saw the value of their stock in Yahoo fall 67 percent, Cisco tumble 75 percent and Sun plunge 90 percent six years later.[6]

Beginning in the fourth quarter of 2005, one stock that was being bought by some very well-known value investors was Pfizer. They were buying Pfizer at a time when the CW was saying the best days of big pharma were behind them; many blockbuster drugs were being replaced by cheaper generics, earnings growth was slowing, and competitors were taking away market share. Value investors instead saw a company that had 14 of the world's 25 best-selling medicines, revenue of $50 billion, and a stock that was trading at a discount to the market and its peers. Given the long-term performance of investors like Marty Whitman (Third Avenue Value) and Bill Miller (Legg Mason Value Trust), would you want to bet against them?

3. *They avoid the latest investment trends.* In 2005, several value funds with excellent long-term performance underperformed the S&P 500. One of the reasons for the lackluster performance was the lack of energy *or* commodity related stocks in their portfolios. While oil prices and most commodity prices soared to new highs, you would have been hard pressed to see many of those companies show up in value investors' portfolios. Value investors purchase shares when the long-term fundamentals make economic sense, not because it is the latest investment fad, and by 2005 it was very fashionable to own energy companies.

What Do You Need?

To be a successful investor, intelligence and hard work alone won't get you there. You need to stick to a discipline and develop the traits described previously. Warren Buffett said at the Berkshire Hathaway Annual Meeting in 2005:

> . . . it all starts with a quality of temperament, not a high IQ. You need an IQ of 125, tops—anything more than that is wasted. But you do need a certain temperament and must be able to think for yourself. Then constantly look for opportunities. You can learn every day. You can't act every day, but you can learn every day. It's like any game, if you enjoy playing it, you'll do well.

The success of many value investors was always based on a combination of hard work and discipline, staying with a proven technique, and paying attention to what constitutes value. In the next and final chapter, I provide you with a summary of the steps you need to follow to become a value investor.

Key Points

1. Track the fundamentals and you will discover an interesting phenomenon. The stock's price will track those fundamentals over the long term, and not the quarterly economic reports. If anything, you're exposed to too much information. You are better off to buy quality companies for the long term; and then, don't open your mail.

2. During the dot-com mania, great companies with solid earnings were "out of favor," and stock prices dropped. At the same time, Internet companies (even those without clearly defined products or profits to report) were soaring, at least for the moment. That should tell you all you need to know—especially when you consider what has become of most of the dot-com companies since the mania.

3. Hard work and intelligence are good traits in any endeavor. But in the market, three tactics help you to succeed. These are: thinking for yourself, discipline, and avoiding the latest flavors of the day in the stock market.

My Final Words of Value

In this chapter, I give you my parting words on the topic of value investing. As I have reminded you consistently throughout the previous chapters, value investing is not brain surgery. You don't need to be hunched over a computer screen watching every wiggle and jiggle of the stock market or staying abreast of every economic report that comes out of Washington. Value investing is really just plain old horse sense: Buy stocks in high-quality companies when they are trading below their underlying worth and then hold onto them. Over time if the business does well, the stock will follow. Most of the heavy lifting on your part will be done before you buy the stock and like everything else in life, the more time and research you put in, the more you will be rewarded.

Read the Annual Reports

I read annual reports of the company I'm looking at and I read the annual reports of the competitors—that is the main source of material.[1]
—Warren Buffett

Rolling up your sleeves and doing some homework is something many investors prefer not to do. It really is not hard to do research, yet I am often surprised how few investors actually do it. It usually requires nothing more than reading the company's annual reports. Warren Buffett's main source of material about a company is the annual reports, which are available free.

After Warren Buffett had graduated from Columbia Business School in 1951, he would leaf through every page of *Moody's* industrial, banks and finance, and public utilities manuals on companies in order to find investment opportunities. He read about an insurance company that had earnings per share of $21 in 1949 and $29 in 1950. The odd thing about it was that the stock itself traded between $4 and $13 . . . *the stock was trading at less than half the earnings per share.* A few pages later he read about National Fire Insurance. The company had $29 in earnings, yet the stock was trading at $27 . . . *you could buy the stock for less than its earnings.* This taught Buffett that Mr. Market sometimes offers you tremendous opportunities right in front of your eyes; you just have to look for them and many times you will find it by reading.

Much has changed over the past half century. There are now sites on the Internet (many of them free) in which you can type in a search criteria and go through more 7,000 stocks to screen out what Buffett and others used to take countless hours to do by hand. Even so, I really question how many investors make use of those sites and find stocks that are trading below their underlying value. In 2003 the big Wall Street firms agreed to a settlement that required them to modify their current stock research departments because of huge conflicts of interest. The banking side of the firms would not stand for a stock analyst publishing a negative company report that could jeopardize millions in investment banking fees, so research reports were not as independent as they appeared. The settlement called for separating the banking side of the business from the research side. It also earmarked funds for independent research firms that cater to retail clients. Unfortunately, most individual investors aren't interested. Why? Perhaps it's much easier to watch CNBC or Bloomberg and hear about the latest stock that is being hyped without taking the time to do any research.

The tools are out there, yet very few take the time to use them. I challenge you to ask two friends who own at least one stock if they read the company's annual report and 10-K prior to buying the stock. I would bet you dollars to donuts that not 1 in 50 will say they did. With the ability to get information on any public company no further than their computer, most investors would prefer not to think. That leaves a lot more opportunities for us.

You can be that 1 in 50 who reads the financial reports. They might not be that exciting, but they are far more informative than any of the financial gurus on television or radio, and you will learn far more. Remember this: Value investing means just that: The search for *value* among a large field of stocks fairly priced or overpriced. They are out there; you only need to look for them and that starts with reading about them.

Principles That Have Stood the Test of Time

> *Ben's principles have remained sound—their value often enhanced*
> *and better understood in the wake of financial storms that*
> *demolished flimsier intellectual structures.*[2]
> *—Warren Buffett writing about Benjamin Graham's book*
> The Intelligent Investor

Don't lose faith in value investing and jump ship to something else simply because your portfolio is lagging over a period of time. You might start reading articles or hearing financial gurus talk about whether stock investors should favor "value" stocks or "growth" stocks. This argument always strikes me as silly. Isn't every investment about value—buying something below its intrinsic value? Should we classify someone who buys an item at a price that is greatly above its intrinsic value a growth investor?

The goal of investing is to buy great businesses at prices that, over time, will produce above-average returns. A stock market investor should look at the profit margins, operating incomes, and the return on equity of a business, regardless of whether it is labeled a "value" or a "growth" stock, and then factor in future earnings growth to determine whether the stock is undervalued or overvalued. Warren Buffett wrote:

> The two approaches are joined at the hip: growth is always a compo-
> nent in the calculation of value. As long as you are buying great com-
> panies for less than their real worth, don't give a darn as to what invest-
> ing style it is called, just watch your account balance rise over time.[3]

Keep in mind that what separates this approach from all others is that it has endured the test of time. At the end of the day it comes down to a few basic principles that haven't changed much since Ben Graham and David Dodd wrote *Security Analysis* and Graham wrote *The Intelligent Investor*.

1. Think of a Stock as Part of a Business

As simple as this sounds, this is the last thing that many investors do. Look at a stock the same way you would look to invest in a private company. Ask yourself:

A. What is the long-term outlook of the business?
B. How good are the people running the business?
C. Is the business attractively priced?

2. Deal with Stock Market Fluctuations

Ben Graham provided a framework for dealing with the stock market that will keep you sane while others are going crazy. Mr. Market is your partner who appears every day and offers to buy or sell your holdings. Some days he is totally depressed and will offer you very low prices. Other days he becomes euphoric and will bid up prices to the sky. He also doesn't mind if you ignore him. Mr. Market is a terrible arbiter of value, so don't allow him to tell you what a company is worth. Take advantage of him when it is to your benefit and ignore him the rest of the time.

3. Keep Three Words in Mind

Warren Buffett said that three words, *margin of safety*, are the most important words on investing. Don't buy $1 worth of assets for 95 cents; wait until the discrepancy between price and value is very wide. Then, and only then, should you make a purchase. The wider the discrepancy between the stock price and the underlying value, the greater the margin of safety.

Invest in Companies with Consistent and Predictable Earnings

> *Experience, however, indicates that the best business returns are usually achieved by companies that are doing something quite similar today to what they were doing five or ten years ago.*[4]
> —*Warren Buffett*

After you have read about the company, and have some understanding about it, stick to those companies that have consistent earnings and revenues. You can't put a good spin on inconsistent results, and it just makes good sense to invest in companies that make money—at a good rate and consistently over time. As a general guideline: Invest in companies with consistent earnings.

On the surface this seems a pretty bland guideline. By following it, investors would have avoided most if not all of the dot-com stocks and companies that stole headlines only to fizzle out and disappear. In order to establish a valuation for a company, it needs to show some kind of earnings. During the heyday of the dot-com boom, many companies were not making money, so Wall Street invented new measures of valuation. One of them was "eyeball count." Internet companies were valued based on how many people went to the site. How this translated to profits, no one ever really figured out.

By looking at companies that have a history of consistent earnings (at least 10 years), you are knocking out a good percentage of companies that are still in their infancy and have no earnings. This then becomes a small universe of stocks to choose from, a very important factor. You will then limit your focus to companies that over periods of time are able to generate earnings above their industry average. Sure, there will be good years and not-so-good years. The main point to keep in mind is consistency. If a company's earnings are very erratic, it is extremely hard to project what future earnings will be and what price to pay for them.

Stick with Quality

Quality companies are easy to spot: Their financial statements are strong. It's impossible for a company to report strong earnings and capitalization each and every year without underlying strength. The success of good management leads to strong competition as well; the better a company's success, the more competitors it will have.

Buffett pointed out in Berkshire Hathaway's 1987 Annual Report that in the Fortune 500 companies, only six reported more than 30 percent return on equity over a decade (based on the *Fortune* 1988 Investor's Guide issue). The most impressive returns are obviously going to be reported by companies whose management has been consistent over time. This is not easy, given ever-changing economic conditions and innovation. Being able to continue succeeding in a dynamic environment is no accident. Only one in four of the *Fortune* list met two important tests of excellence: more than 30 percent return on equity over a decade *and* no single years with returns under 15 percent.

The companies on the list of exceptional results had two important attributes that will surprise many people. First, they tended to use very little debt capital, showing that well-run businesses do not need to borrow. Second, the list consisted of some rather mundane companies (all but one of them were high-tech companies or drug manufacturers), selling products or offering services that did not change much over the reported decade.

Return on Equity (ROE)

Where you find a company that is able to produce a high ROE year after year, you will surely find a great business. The business world is highly competitive; Charles Darwin could have been speaking about it when he lectured on survival of the fittest. If a company is selling a product or service that has customers beating a path to their door, it won't be long until that company faces a host of competitors.

A company that is able to consistently increase the worth of the business (shareholder equity) and at the same time increase profits (net income) is rare indeed. A business that is able to produce an ROE (while using little debt) greater than 15 percent are the ones that should garner most of your attention.

Margins

When your third grade teacher told you to "watch the margins" when you are writing a composition, she was giving you excellent investment advice. The ability to expand margins, operating and net profit, is a hallmark of a quality company.

Businesses that have rising operating margins are making more money on every dollar of sales. As time goes on, quality businesses are able to boost operating margins as they become more efficient as they grow. If a retailer with 10 stores has one warehouse, they will spread the expense over each one of their stores, or 1/10 of the cost per store. But when that same retailer grows to 50 stores (assuming that they won't need another warehouse), they will now be able to spread the expense of the warehouse over 50 stores, or 1/50 of the cost per store. The same goes for advertising, labor, trucking, and so on. The bigger they get, the more they should be able to earn due to economies of scale.

At the end of the day, they should see a rise in their net profit margin, or the profits that fall to the bottom line. A business that is able to expand their net profit margin on a consistent basis is keeping a tight watch on expenses, is not sacrificing profit for sales and most likely is a leader in their industry.

Investing in quality companies allows you to sleep better at night. There will be times when the stock of a quality company will sell off sharply. During these sell-offs you should discern if the drop in stock price is a function of Mr. Market or the fundamentals of the company. Those are the times you will be able to get your biggest bargains.

Go Large Caps

> *A great business at a fair price is superior to a fair business at a great price.*
> —*Charlie Munger*

While your universe of quality companies might number in the hundreds, I recommend that you start out focusing on large-cap companies. Most investors define a large cap as a company with a market capitalization greater than $10 billion. If you fish in this pond, you will be selecting from the high-quality pool of great companies. As you gain more confidence you can expand your universe to include mid-cap (market capitalizations $1 billion to $10 billion) and small caps (market caps less than $1 billion) if you so desire.

Benjamin Graham made a great case for investing in large-cap companies:

> "...concentrate on the larger companies that are going through a period of unpopularity. While small companies may also be under-valued for similar reasons, and in many cases may later increase their earnings and share price, they entail the risk of a definitive loss of prof-itability and also of protracted neglect by the market in spite of better earnings. The large companies thus have a double advantage over the others. First, they have the resources in capital and brain power to carry them through adversity and back to a satisfactory earnings base. Second, the market is likely to respond with reasonable speed to any improvement shown."[5]

Some value investors feel that large-cap stocks are too "pawed over" by analysts and that they are more efficiently priced than mid- and small-cap stocks. They feel you can't get high returns from this segment of the market. I wanted to see if this prejudice from looking at large caps was myth or reality. Looking back over the past 5 years, I selected the largest market cap companies that had their stock price rise greater than 35 percent. Other than 2002, I listed the top 10 by year. In other words, I wanted to see if these elephants could tap-dance. The results surprised me. See Table 11.1.

> *You might think that institutions, with their large staffs of highly-paid and experienced investment professionals, would be a force for stability and reason in financial markets. They are not: stocks heavily owned and constantly monitored by institutions have often been among the most inappropriately valued.*[6]
> —*Warren Buffett*

Most of these companies are household names (Nissan Motor, Citigroup, ExxonMobil) and not obscure large caps that didn't garner attention. The con-ventional wisdom said that the stocks of large caps don't increase by a large percentage in any one year because they are too big. Yet $22 billion market cap Boston Scientific increased 76 percent (2002), $110 billion market cap Intel rose 107 percent (2003), $75 billion market cap Apple soared 201 percent (2004),

TABLE 11.1 Elephants That Can Tap Dance

Company	Ticker	Total Return 2002	Market Cap $ (Millions)
Nissan Motor ADR	NSANY	45%	46,910
Halliburton Co.	HAL	47%	31,889
Boston Scientific	BSX	76%	22,792
Zimmer Holdings	ZMH	36%	20,232

Company	Ticker	Total Return 2003	Market Cap $ (Millions)
Citigroup Inc.	C	42%	248,140
Altria Group	MO	43%	180,133
JPMorgan Chase	JPM	60%	169,007
Vodafone Group ADR	VOD	40%	161,873
Cisco Systems	CSCO	85%	158,155
Chevron Corp.	CVX	35%	149,242
BHP Billiton Ltd. ADR	BHP	62%	127,511
ConocoPhillips	COP	40%	111,205
Intel Corp.	INTC	107%	110,726
Telefonica SA ADR	TEF	73%	103,524

Company	Ticker	Total Return 2004	Market Cap $ (Millions)
Google, Inc.	GOOG	92%	37,283
ConocoPhillips	COP	36%	111,205
Petroleo Brasileiro ADR	PBR	43%	97,921
Apple Inc.	AAPL	201%	75,699
UnitedHealth Group	UNH	51%	71,622
Qualcomm Inc.	QCOM	58%	66,597
Tyco Int'l Ltd.	TYC	35%	61,351
Sprint Nextel Corp.	S	55%	56,666
Ericsson ADR	ERIC	78%	55,287
Manulife Fin'l	MFC	46%	53,381

Company	Ticker	Total Return 2005	Market Cap $ (Millions)
Google, Inc.	GOOG	115%	144,475
BHP Billiton Ltd. ADR	BHP	40%	127,511
ConocoPhillips	COP	37%	111,205
Hewlett-Packard	HPQ	38%	110,018
Petroleo Brasileiro ADR	PBR	84%	97,921

(Continued)

TABLE 11.1	Elephants That Can Tap Dance (*Continued*)		
Company	Ticker	Total Return 2005	Market Cap $ (Millions)
Genentech Inc.	DNA	70%	85,522
Schlumberger Ltd.	SLB	46%	77,385
Apple Inc.	AAPL	123%	75,699
Royal Bank of Canada	RY.TO	46%	72,570
UnitedHealth Group	UNH	41%	71,622
Company	Ticker	Total Return 2006	Market Cap $ (Millions)
ExxonMobil Corp.	XOM	39%	419,029
Vodafone Group ADR	VOD	36%	161,873
Cisco Systems	CSCO	60%	158,155
AT&T Inc.	T	53%	141,732
Hewlett-Packard	HPQ	45%	110,018
Telefonica SA ADR	TEF	47%	103,524
Petroleo Brasileiro ADR	PBR	51%	97,921
Merck & Co.	MRK	43%	96,375
Oracle Corp.	ORCL	40%	86,421
Goldman Sachs	GS	57%	85,756
Comcast Corp.	CMCSK	63%	80,853

Companies with market caps greater than $20 billion and rose more than 35% in a given year.
Source: Value Line Investment Survey.

$144 billion market cap Google was up 115 percent (2005), and $80 billion market cap Comcast rocketed 63 percent (2006).

The point of this screen was to impress upon me that large caps are not as efficiently priced as many would have you believe. These elephants not only can tap-dance, they can also run sprints with their smaller-cap cousins.

Able Leaders

I have found in my 40-year career on Wall Street that managements that are inconsistent, unwilling to judge their performance against previously stated objectives and are too focused on temporary fixes cannot serve as the appropriate catalyst for desperately needed changes that troubled companies need to initiate.[7]

—*Robert A. Olstein*

In addition to checking out the company, make sure you know who is running the show. In other words, know the jockey as well as the horse. A good company in the hands of a great manager creates a lot of value-added for shareholders. Unfortunately, when looking to invest in a company, many investors don't take the time to research the management. People will invest considerable amounts of money buying shares of a company and not even know the name of the CEO, and that doesn't make a whole lot of sense to me.

You are now a shareholder, and your fortunes will rise and fall with the success or failure of the company. One of the first things you should look for when researching management is how shareholder friendly they are. Do they look at shareholders as partners? Are they increasing shareholder value by buying back their shares, or increasing their dividends? What percent of the stock does management own? You should have confidence that management and you are in the same boat and that they have a vested interest in increasing the worth of the business.

Competitive Advantage

Knowing what a company's competitive advantage is and how long it will endure can steer you away from mediocre companies and keep you focused on the truly quality companies. One of the first questions you should ask as you begin reading the annual reports is: Out of all the companies in this industry, why does this one stand out? If you can't come up with a reason that includes the strength of the company's brand, captive customer base (switching), lowest-cost producer, or protected market or product (permits, patents or government protection), you should move on.

When looking at a company for a possible investment, Buffett says to himself, Give me a billion dollars and how much can I hurt the guy?[8] If you can't answer the question, you are looking at a great company. Think about it, if you had $1 billion, would you be able to dent UPS and their vast network, experience, and know-how? In 2006 they delivered more than 15 million packages; can you do it better, cheaper, and faster? If you had $5 billion, would you be able to convince patients and doctors to switch to your brand of coronary stents and other biomedical devices? You also need to factor in the years of research it would take to get Food and Drug Administration (FDA) approval for your products. Medtronics and UPS are just two examples of companies that have very strong competitive advantages.

When you compare the return on equity and net profit margin against the company's industry, you most likely will find that the company has a higher ROE and/or net profit margin. A company that dominates its industry and has management that is determined to continue to increase market share is the kind of company that you should own.

The Right Price to Pay

> *In investments, there's no such thing as a called strike. You can stand there at the plate and the pitcher can throw a ball right down the middle, and if it's General Motors at 47 and you don't know enough to decide on General Motors at 47, you let it go right on by and no one's going to call a strike. The only way you can have a strike is to swing and miss.*[9]
> —*Warren Buffett*

After selecting the company, determining the price to pay for it will have the biggest effect on your returns. The point here is you want to invest only when the odds of an adequate return are in your favor; otherwise it is best to wait. When projecting future earnings per share (EPS) growth and the P/E ratio, keep in mind to factor in a margin of safety. Buffett considers the margin of safety principle "to be the cornerstone of investment success."[10] If you factored in a low projection for EPS growth and P/E ratio and the company exceeds those numbers over the next five years, you essentially hit the jackpot. Upside surprises are also great; just don't count on their happening.

Starbucks' current price is $30 per share, the trailing 12 months' EPS is $0.77, the past five years' EPS growth was 25 percent, and they are currently trading at a P/E ratio of 40. Over the long term, studies have shown that no more than a handful of companies are able to grow their EPS greater than 15 percent, let alone Starbucks' 25 percent growth.

Since we know the importance of factoring in a margin of safety, we will assume projected EPS over the next 5 years will be 15 percent and the P/E ratio will come down to earth at 17. Five years pass and Starbucks matches our projections. Our return on investment will be determined by the price we paid for the stock today. See Table 11.2.

If we couldn't have waited to own Starbucks and went out and bought it at $30 per share, our return on investment (ROI) would be negative over five years. In fact the stock price has to fall to $18 per share for us to beat money market returns. In order to get adequately rewarded for buying the stock, we would need to wait until Starbucks falls from its current price of $30 to about $14 per share. In other words, Starbucks would have to fall by more than 50 percent from its current price to attract your interest!

TABLE 11.2 The Price You Pay Determines Your Return	
Stock Price Paid in 2007	5 Year ROI
$30.00	−2.6%
$26.00	0.3%
$22.00	3.7%
$18.00	7.9%
$14.50	12.5%
$13.00	15.0%

Note: Assumes 15% EPS and P/E of 17 over 5 years.

That is why great value investors keep the bat on their shoulder and swing only at the "fat pitches." Think the way Buffett does when he says that "the stock market is a no-called-strike game. You don't have to swing at everything—you can wait for your pitch."[11] Determine the price to pay that includes a margin of safety and act only when the price is trading at your desired rate of return.

The Right Temperament

> It's all simple, it's not rocket science. It's Wall Street that makes it complicated. What Max Heine and Warren Buffett did was to boil it all down to buying companies when their value was deeply discounted . . .[12]
> —*Michael Price*

While the concept of value investing is buying companies trading below their underlying value, actually putting it into practice is the challenge most investors face. Several times I have mentioned in this book that while you need some brain power, the real key is having the right temperament. As a value investor, you will most likely be buying stocks when they are closer to their yearly lows than highs, which is not an easy thing to do. You will also be making a purchase in a company that is either neglected, has negative press swirling around its head, had a sharp decline in its stock price—or all of the above.

That is where temperament comes into play. You must let the facts determine the price of the company and not Mr. Market. That means separating yourself from the crowd, challenging the conventional wisdom, and avoiding Wall Street's latest "sector love affair." There will be times when you will look silly by owning something that "everybody knows" is a loser. But those are the times when bargains exist and according to Benjamin Graham, that is when you have the edge.

> The investor who permits himself to be stampeded or unduly worried by unjustified market declines in his holdings is perversely transforming his basic advantage into a basic disadvantage. That man would be better off if his stocks had no market quotation at all, for he would then be spared the mental anguish caused him by *other persons'* mistakes of judgment.[13]

Buy a stock like you are buying a private company: Look at the fundamentals of the company (earnings, sales, net profit margins, etc.) and not the stock price to determine how well the company is doing. Over the long run, you will be much happier and richer.

Have Patience

> *Investing is where you find a few great companies and then sit on your ass.*[14]
> —*Charlie Munger*

Instead of holding onto great companies for the long haul, most investors do the exact opposite, continually trading in and out of stocks. Frequent trading is a very difficult game to win. When you factor in commission costs, the spread between the bid and ask, and taxes (short-term capital gains), there is a lot of friction eating away at your returns. In addition, you really have to be right many more times than you are wrong in order to make money.

The reason to sell a stock should have nothing to do with the stock market. The goal should be to hang on for as long as possible. Only after examining the business fundamentals of a company and deciding that they no longer meet certain requirements for holding them should you sell. If an investor bought $1,000 worth of Starbucks in 1992, it would now be worth close to $40,000. I know it's not easy to find great companies and even more difficult to hold onto them when Mr. Market drives their price lower. But the rewards are that much greater when you stick with it.

Common Sense

> *Not everything that can be counted counts*
> *and not everything that counts can be counted.*
> —*Albert Einstein*

Investing is part art and part science. The science part is easy; all you need to do is look at the numbers. Review the company's balance sheet, income statement, and cash flow and you are halfway there. However, if successful investing were all about the numbers and reading, accountants and librarians would be the highest paying occupations. Such is not always the case.

The art part comes into play when after reading a company's annual report and the letter to shareholders, you ask yourself the following: How does the company plan on expanding the business? What challenges does it see in the future? Is it hungry? Has the CEO climbed to the peak and fallen asleep? You can never get those insights just from the numbers. A good investor has to be an investigative reporter. If the industry is changing and the company is starting to lose market share, dig down deep and find out if the problems are temporary or long term. If temporary, hold on but if there is a long term problem, be prepared to sell and find a better investment.

Many great companies suffered problems that were only temporary and other problems that were long term. You must be able to distinguish between the two. Financial statements can tell you only where a company has been. Keeping a sharp eye out and listening hard will tell you where a company is going and if their problems are just speed bumps or devastating potholes. There really is nothing magic about stock success. It takes work, a business mentality and approach, and a respect for the numbers.

Conclusion

That's all there is to it. If you stick with a philosophy that looks at stocks as pieces of a company, ignore the daily ups and downs of the stock market, give yourself a wide margin of safety, and buy companies with strong financials, it's hard to mess up.

Keep in mind that Wall Street likes to make things as complex as possible. Investing isn't that hard, it just requires you to stick to a few principles, keep your head while others around you are losing theirs, and wait for your price.

Use the worksheet (Table 11.3) when researching a company.

TABLE 11.3 Value Investing Worksheet

Company _____

Symbol _____

Industry _____

CEO _____

Year took office _____

Annual Reports

	Current	2 years ago	3 years ago	4 years ago	5 years ago
Read	Y-N	Y-N	Y-N	Y-N	Y-N

Competitive Advantage

Company moat	Brand	Switching	Cost	Protected	Other
	Y-N	Y-N	Y-N	Y-N	Y-N
How likely will moat endure over next 5 years?	Very likely	Highly likely	Not Likely	Not sure	

Competitors

	Competitor #1	Competitor #2	Competitor #3
Read current annual report?	Y-N	Y-N	Y-N

What is the biggest risk to the company over next 5 years? _____

Probability of it happening?
0% (nil)–100% (certain) _____

Financial Checklist

	Company	5-year Trend	Industry	5-year Trend
5 Year ESP Growth	%	Rise–Fall–Flat	%	Rise–Fall–Flat
5 Year Revenue Growth	%	Rise–Fall–Flat	%	Rise–Fall–Flat
Current net profit margin	%	Rise–Fall–Flat	%	Rise–Fall–Flat
Current ROE	%	Rise–Fall–Flat	%	Rise–Fall–Flat
% Long-term debt to equity	%	Rise–Fall–Flat	%	Rise–Fall–Flat

Warren Buffett summed up stock investing by saying that:

Stocks are simple. All you do is buy shares in a great business for less than the business is intrinsically worth, with managers of the highest integrity and ability. Then you own those shares forever.[15]

I couldn't have said it any better.

The wonderful business—you can figure what will happen, you can't figure out when it will happen. You don't want to focus too much on when but you want to focus on what. If you are right about what, you don't have to worry about when very much.[16]

—*Warren Buffett*

Glossary

annual report a booklet prepared by management that describes the financial condition and company operations, which is distributed to all shareholders on a yearly basis.

bottom-up approach a method of identifying investment opportunities one at a time through analysis of financial statements and the outlook of the company.

dividend payout ratio the percentage of earnings paid in cash to shareholders. It is calculated by dividing the dividends paid by the earnings per share.

DJIA an index of 30 stocks traded on the public exchanges. It is the most widely known index and is used as a measure of the health and direction of the overall stock market.

economic moat a term coined by Warren Buffett referring to the competitive advantage a company has over its competitors. The moat acts as a barrier against other companies trying to gain market share.

efficient market theory (EMT) a theory that states all information about a company is already reflected in the price of the stock, which is why one can not outperform the stock market. Luck explains why some investors beat the stock market; skill is not a factor.

footnotes provide details for the numbers that appear in the company's financial statements. Supposed to provide a better understanding of a particular number.

Form 10-K audited report filed annually with the Securities and Exchange Commission. Similar to the shareholder annual report but provides more detailed financial and nonfinancial information.

free cash flow (FCF) the cash left over after paying all its expenses and investing for its growth.

money managers in return for a fee, persons responsible for buying and selling a portfolio of securities.

Mr. Market a metaphor created by Benjamin Graham to demonstrate the erratic price swings of the stock market. Based on Mr. Market's "moods" he can be euphoric (bid prices higher) one day and be depressed (drive prices lower) the next.

net profit margin (NPM) a measure of how profitable a company is after all expenses and taxes are paid. It is derived by dividing net income by total sales or revenue. It is expressed as a percentage and makes comparison between different companies much easier.

PE ratio   a stock's market price divided by its current earnings per share. The PE ratio is used by investors as a fundamental measure of the attractiveness of a particular security versus all other securities. The lower the ratio relative to the average of the share market, the lower the market's profit growth expectations.

program trading   trades where 15 or more stocks are traded in order to capture small price discrepancies among stocks, options, and futures.

proxy statement   information provided by management to shareholders so they can vote in an informed manner at annual shareholders' meetings. Also lists total compensation paid to company executives.

random walk theory   a theory that stock prices move randomly and unpredictably. Fundamental analysis is a waste of time since no one can forecast stock prices.

return on equity (ROE)   a measure of how profitable a company is. It is derived by dividing net income by total shareholder equity. ROE tells shareholders how effective management is in deploying their money. It is expressed as a percentage and makes comparison between different companies much easier.

Securities and Exchange Commission (SEC)   the federal agency responsible for oversight of publicly listed corporations, and for enforcing laws and regulations at the federal level.

top-down approach   a method of identifying investment opportunities by making a prediction about the future, determining the investment consequence, and then selecting the proper security.

transparency   disclosure of a company's financial reporting so investors can get a more accurate understanding of the financial condition of the company.

value investing   a method of determining the value of a business and then buying shares at a discount from that value.

Recommended Reading and Resources

Value Investing

Browne, Christopher. *The Little Book of Value Investing*. Hoboken, NJ: John Wiley & Sons, 2006.

Dorsey, Pat. *The Five Rules for Successful Stock Investing*. Hoboken, NJ: John Wiley & Sons, 2004.

Ellis, Charles D. *The Investor's Anthology*. Hoboken, NJ: John Wiley & Sons, 1997.

Greenblatt, Joel. *The Little Book That Beats the Market*. Hoboken, NJ: John Wiley & Sons, 2006.

Greenwald, Bruce, and Judd Kahn. *Competition Demystified*. New York, NY: Penguin Group, 2005.

Greenwald, Bruce, and Judd Kahn. *Value Investing: From Graham to Buffett and Beyond*. Hoboken, NJ: John Wiley & Sons, 2001.

Accounting and Annual Reports

Graham, Benjamin (New Introduction by Michael F. Price). *The Interpretation of Financial Statements*. New York, NY: First HarperBusiness. 1998.

Leder, Michelle. *Financial Fine Print: Uncovering a Company's True Value*. Hoboken, NJ: John Wiley & Sons, 2003.

Stanko, Brian, and Thomas Zeller. *Understanding Corporate Annual Reports: A User's Guide*. Hoboken, NJ: John Wiley & Sons, 2003.

Thomsett, Michael C. *Annual Reports 101*. New York, NY: Amacom, 2007.

Benjamin Graham

Graham, Benjamin (updated with new commentary by Jason Zweig). *The Intelligent Investor*. New York, NY: HarperBusiness Essentials, 2003.

Lowe, Janet. *Benjamin Graham on Value Investing*. Chicago, IL: Dearborn Financial Publishing, Inc., 1994.

———. *Value Investing Made Easy*. New York, NY: McGraw-Hill, 1996.

Warren Buffett

Altucher, James. *Trade Like Warren Buffett*. Hoboken, NJ: John Wiley & Sons, 2005.
Cunningham, Lawrence A. *The Essays of Warren Buffett: Lessons for Corporate America*. New York, NY: The Cunningham Group, 1st rev. ed., 2001.
Lowe, Janet. *Warren Buffett Speaks*. Hoboken, NJ: John Wiley & Sons, 1997.
Hagstrom, Robert G. *The Essential Buffett*. Hoboken, NJ: John Wiley & Sons, 2001,
———. *The Warren Buffett Portfolio*. Hoboken, NJ: John Wiley & Sons, 1999.
———. *The Warren Buffett Way*. Hoboken, NJ: John Wiley & Sons, 2005.
Kilpatrick, Andrew. *Of Permanent Value: The Story of Warren Buffett/2007 International Edition* in 2 vol. Birmingham, AL: AKPE Publishing, 2007.
Lowenstein, Rodger. *Buffett: The Making of an American Capitalist*. New York, NY: Doubleday Dell Publishing Group, 1995.
O'Loughlin, James. *The Real Warren Buffett: Managing Capital, Leading People*. London, England: Nicholas Brealey Publishing, 2004.
Vick, Timothy. *How to Pick Stocks Like Warren Buffett*. New York, NY: McGraw-Hill, 2001.

Charlie Munger

Kaufman, Peter D. *Poor Charlie's Almanack*. Virginia Beach, VA: PCA Publication, LLC, 2005.
Lowe, Janet. *Damn Right*. Hoboken, NJ: John Wiley & Sons, 2000.

Resources

Berkshire Hathaway: www.berkshirehathaway.com.
   Warren Buffett's Letters to Berkshire Shareholders 1997–2007.
Wesco Financial Corporation: http://www.wescofinancial.com/
   Charles T. Munger's Letters to Wesco Shareholders.
Securities and Exchange Commission: http://www.sec.gov/edgar.shtml
   Search capabilities for all SEC filings by company and filing.
Annual report resource center: www.irin.com.
   5 years of most companies annual reports in PDF format.
   Also can request hard copies mailed to you.

Executive Disclosure.com: http://www.executivedisclosure.com/
   Online database that provides compensation data for officers and directors of
   publicly traded companies.
Footnoted.org: www.Footnoted.org.
   Freelance journalist Michelle Leder systematically takes apart proxy state-
   ments, quarterlies, and news releases, offering opinions and asking questions
   about management compensation and other items tucked away in the small
   print.
Corporate History: http://www.fundinguniverse.com/company-histories/
Corporate history on thousands of companies.

Stock Data

ADVFN Financials: http://www.advfn.com/
   Extensive financial information on publicly traded companies.
Google Finance: http://finance.google.com/finance
   Extensive information on any publicly traded company.
Money Central: www.moneycentral.com.
   MSN's financial web site, offers Guided Research on any stock.
Morningstar: www.morningstar.com (membership required).
   Morningstar stock analysts reports on 1,900 stocks.
Value Line: www.valueline.com (membership required).
   Large independent research staffs of investment analysts and statisticians.
   Best known for *The Value Line Investment Survey*, which covers 1,700
   stocks.

Educational Resources

Conscious Investor: www.consciousinvestor.com (Membership required).
Offers software to screen investment grade companies and calculate the buying
   prices.
GuruFocus.com: www.gurufocus.com.
GuruFocus tracks the Stock Picks and Portfolio Holdings of Warren Buffett, and
   other guru investors.
Hidden Values Alert: www.hiddenvaluesalert.com.
   The author's newsletter on value investing. Includes monthly articles on value
   investing, stock selections and three different portfolios.

The 15 Percent Delusion

We have held the opinion for years that Carol Loomis of *Fortune* Magazine is one of the finest financial reporters of our era. We would like to recommend two of her recent articles. In the February 5, 2001, article, "The 15% Delusion," she writes that "serial grandstanding about goals and targets has somehow become accepted executive behavior. The most common goal articulated among good-sized companies is annual growth in earnings per share of 15%." However, citing two studies, she points out how rare it is that large companies actually succeed in achieving 15% growth over long periods of time.

In our opinion, investors should be very wary of falling for the touted "15% (or 20%) delusion" and paying prices for stocks predicated on assumed future growth rates that are highly unlikely to be realized over the long term. Investors should also be wary of the quality of earnings of these companies, which may go to all lengths in order to sustain the "15% delusion" for as long as possible. Ms. Loomis elaborates:

The record shows that ambitious goals often combined with incentive compensation plans that encourage unwise behavior, have time and time again led corporations to "manage" earnings in unfortunate ways. Sometimes their behavior is simply uneconomical, as when they aggressively peddle cut price merchandise at the end of a quarter, thereby stealing from full-price business down the road. Or they may use capital poorly, buying themselves earnings in the short run but creaming their returns on capital. Worse, they may cook the books, letting their zeal for making the numbers push them over the legal line.

—Sequoia Fund, Inc., Annual Report, December 31, 2000

Notes

INTRODUCTION   Value Really Means Something

1. Warren E. Buffett, "The Superinvestors of Graham-and-Doddsville," *Hermes*, Columbia Business School, New York, 1984.
2. http://acct.tamu.edu/giroux/financial.html.
3. Peter Lynch and John Rothchild, *One Up on Wall Street* (New York: Simon & Schuster, 1989): 74.
4. Berkshire Hathaway Annual Report, 1988.
5. Buffett, "Superinvestors."

CHAPTER 1   The 5 Misconceptions of Value Investing

1. Berkshire Hathaway Annual Report, 1992.
2. John C. Bogle, *The Battle for the Soul of Capitalism* (New Haven, CT: Yale University Press, 2005).
3. Peter Lynch, *Beating the Street* (New York: Simon & Schuster, 1993): 340.
4. Benjamin Graham, *The Intelligent Investor*, 4th ed. (New York: Harper & Row, 1973): 273.
5. http://www.nfl.com/draft/analysis/expert/brandt/te.
6. *Outstanding Investor Digest*, August 8, 1996, 29.
7. Warren E. Buffett, "The Superinvestors of Graham-and-Doddsville," *Hermes*, Columbia Business School, New York, 1984.
8. Berkshire Hathaway Annual Report, 1992.

CHAPTER 2   The Basics of Value Investing: A Few Things You Must Know

1. Louis Lowenstein, "Searching for Rational Investors in a Perfect Storm" (Columbia Law School, The Center for Law and Economic Studies, working paper No. 255, July 17, 2004).
2. Berkshire Hathaway Annual Report, 1988.

3. Berkshire Hathaway Annual Meeting, 1997.

4. Lowenstein, "Searching for Rational Investors."

5. Longleaf Partners Funds, Annual Report for 1999.

6. John C. Bogle, *The Battle for the Soul of Capitalism* (New Haven, CT: Yale University Press, 2005):74.

7. Berkshire Hathaway Annual Report, 1978.

8. Anuj Gangahar, "JP Morgan Takes Lead in Hedge Funds," *Financial Times*, March 6, 2007, 18.

9. Berkshire Hathaway Annual Report, 1987.

10. Seth Klarman, *Margin of Safety* (New York: HarperBusiness, 1991).

CHAPTER 3   Market Caveats: Lessons from the Past

1. Benjamin Graham, *The Intelligent Investor*, updated with new commentary by Jason Zweig (New York: HarperBusiness Essentials, 2003): 217.

2. Benjamin Graham, *The Intelligent Investor*, 4th ed. (New York: Harper & Row, 1973): xv.

3. Haywood Kelly, "A Quick Q&A with Warren Buffett," Morningstar, May 6, 1998.

4. Berkshire Hathaway, Letters to Shareholders, 1987.

5. Andrew Carnegie, "Wealth," *North American Review* 148 (June 1889): 653–664.

6. Carnegie said this in his essay, "How to Succeed in Life" (1903), and although he made it famous, he borrowed it from Mark Twain in "Pudd'nhead Wilson's Calendar" (Chapter 15), 1894.

7. John Maynard Keynes, personal letter to F.C. Scott, August 15, 1934.

8. Buffett was quoting Broadway impresario Billy Rose.

9. Philip A. Fisher, *Common Stocks and Uncommon Profits* (Hoboken, NJ: John Wiley & Sons, 2003): 108.

10. Martin Whitman and Martin Shubik, *The Aggressive Conservative Investor* (Hoboken, NJ: John Wiley & Sons, 2006): xxviii.

11. Berkshire Hathaway Annual Report, 1993.

12. Warren Buffett speaking with MBA students, Florida State University, 1998.

13. Graham, *Intelligent Investor*, 4th ed.

14. Peter Lynch, *Beating the Street* (New York: Simon & Schuster, 1993): 27.

15. Berkshire Hathaway Annual Report, 1994.

16. Padraic Cassidy, "Oak Value Fund Upbeat on Berkshire Hathaway, Oracle, Capital One Financial," www.marketwatch.com, February 28, 2007.

CHAPTER 4   Are Great Companies Great Investments? Stick with the Champs

1. Jeff Anderson and Gary Smith, "A Great Company Can Be a Great Investment," *Financial Analysts Journal* 62, no. 4 (July/August 2006): 86–93.

2. Ibid.

3. Berkshire Hathaway, Annual Report, 1989.

4. Ibid.

5. Berkshire Hathaway, Annual Report, 1981.

6. Berkshire Hathaway, Annual Meeting, 2000.

CHAPTER 5   Who's in Charge? Management Counts: Getting Comfortable with Management

1. Benjamin Graham, *The Intelligent Investor*, 4th ed. (New York: Harper & Row, 1973): 110.

2. http://en.wikipedia.org/wiki/Regulation_FD.

3. http://www.sec.gov/news/headlines/xeroxsettles.htm.

4. www.Heartlandexpress.com, "Our Story."

5. Heartland Express, Inc. SEC filing DEF14A, April 6,2006, www.sec.gov.

6. Ibid.

7. SEC Form 10-K, December 31, 2006.

8. Nicholas Kristof, "Captains of Piracy," *New York Times*, March 21, 2005.

9. www.footnoted.org, Morgan Stanley SEC Form DEF 14A, February 24, 2006, 19.

10. www.footnoted.org, Aaron Rent Inc. SEC Form DEF 14A—Other definitive proxy statements, April 7, 2006, 15.

11. Wellpoint Inc., SEC Form DEF 14A—Other definitive proxy statements, April 13, 2006, 15.

12. Marc Ballon, "The Cheapest CEO in America," *Inc.*, October 1977.

13. http://www.investor.reuters.wallst.com/stocks/Ratios.asp?rpc=66 &ticker=FAST.O 12/12/06.

14. Sam Walton and John Huey, *Sam Walton: Made in America* (New York: Bantam, 1993): 83.

15. Tom Brown, *Bank Director Magazine*, 4Q05, http://www.bankdirector.com/issues/articles.pl?article_id=11730.

16. Mary Buffett, and David Clark, *The Tao of Warren Buffett* (New York: Scribner's, 2006): 37.

17. Based on notes from Brian Zen, CFA, New York Society of Security Analysts, February 16, 2006.

18. Berkshire Hathaway Annual Report, 1980.

CHAPTER 6 Competition: Threat or Opportunity? The Enduring Competitive Advantage

1. In Michael Sincere, *101 Investment Lessons from the Wizards of Wall Street* (Franklin Lakes, NJ: Career Press, 1999): 99.

2. Michael J Mauboussin, *More Than You Know* (New York: Columbia University Press, 2006): 60.

3. *American Workplace in a Global Economy: Factbook on U.S. Workplace Trends*, 2004.

4. Janet Lowe, *Warren Buffett Speaks* (New York: John Wiley & Sons, 1997): 126.

5. Berkshire Hathaway Annual Report, 1995.

6. Warren Buffett and Carol Loomis, "Mr. Buffett on the Stock Market," *Fortune*, November 22, 1999.

7. "The 100 Top Brands," *BusinessWeek*, August 7, 2006, 60.

8. Paul Taylor, "Apple Remains Unfazed by March of Microsoft's Zune," *Financial Times*, December 28, 2006, 10.

9. NPD TechWorld, March 1993–2004, based on total U.S. retail sales.

CHAPTER 7 The Essential Valuation Variables That Really Count: Part 1—Financial Statement Basics

1. Benjamin Graham, "The New Speculation in Common Stocks," *Analysts Journal*, 1958.

2. Janet Lowe, *Warren Buffett Speaks* (New York: John Wiley & Sons, 1997): 128.

3. Robert G. Hagstrom, *The Warren Buffett Way*, 2d ed. (Hoboken, NJ: John Wiley & Sons, 2005).

CHAPTER 8   The Essential Operating Variables That Really Count: Part 2—Bringing the Numbers to Life

1. Berkshire Hathaway Annual Report, 1998.
2. Berkshire Hathaway Annual Report, 1996.
3. Berkshire Hathaway Annual Meeting, 1998.

CHAPTER 9   The Price of Stock versus the Value of the Company

1. Benjamin Graham, *The Intelligent Investor*, 4th ed., New York, NY: Harper & Row Publishers, 1973, 109.
2. Ibid.
3. Berkshire Hathaway Annual Report, 1996.
4. Andy Serwer, "The Oracle of Everything," *Fortune*, November 2, 2002.
5. James J. Cramer, "The Winners of the New World," The Street.com, February 29, 2000.
6. Janet Lowe, *Warren Buffett Speaks* (New York: John Wiley & Sons, 1997): 128.
7. Peter D. Kaufman, *Poor Charlie's Almanack* (Virginia Beach, VA: PCA Publications, 2005): 57.
8. Bruce Greenwald, Judd Kahn, Paul Sonkin, and Michael van Biema, *Value Investing from Graham to Buffett and Beyond* (Hoboken, NJ: Wiley Finance, 2001): 3–4.
9. Ibid., 14 (loosely interpreted).
10. Ibid., 14.
11. Tweedy, Browne Company LP, "What Has Worked in Investing: Studies of Investment Approaches and Characteristics Associated with Exceptional Returns," 1992.
12. Berkshire Hathaway Annual Report, 1994.
13. Ibid.
14. Berkshire Hathaway Annual Report, 1996.
15. See page 176 for discussion of Carol J. Loomis, "The 15% Delusion," *Fortune*, February 5, 2001.
16. Timothy Vick, *How to Pick Stocks Like Warren Buffett* (New York: McGraw-Hill, 2001): 148.
17. Berkshire Hathaway Annual Report, Letter to Shareholders, 1974.
18. John C. Bogle, "The Amazing Disappearance of the Individual Investor," *Wall Street Journal*, October 3, 2005.

19. Week of December 26–29, 2006 (NYSE Program Trading Statistics, www.nyse.com).

20. Berkshire Hathaway Annual Report, 1991.

CHAPTER 10   Your Own Worst Enemy

1. Benjamin Graham, *The Intelligent Investor*, 4th ed. (New York: Harper & Row, 1973): 273.

2. Diya Gullapalli and Shefali Anand, "Fund Stars Don't Like This Ride," *Wall Street Journal*, January 13, 2006, sec. C1.

3. Legg Mason Value Trust Inc., investment commentary and quarterly report to shareholders for 2005, ii.

4. William Shakespeare, *Julius Caesar*, I, ii, 140–141.

5. Through April 26, 2006.

6. From March 27, 2000, through April 26, 2006.

CHAPTER 11   My Final Words of Value

1. Janet Lowe, *Warren Buffett Speaks* (New York: John Wiley & Sons, 1997): 121.

2. Warren Buffett, "Benjamin Graham 1894–1976," *Financial Analysts Journal*, November/December 1976.

3. Berkshire Hathaway Annual Report, 1992.

4. Berkshire Hathaway Annual Report, 1987.

5. Benjamin Graham, *The Intelligent Investor*, 4th ed. (New York: Harper & Row, 1973): 79.

6. Berkshire Hathaway Annual Report 1985.

7. Olstein All Cap Value Fund, Letter to Shareholders, Semi-Annual Report, December 31, 2006.

8. Warren Buffett, Florida speech 1998 transcript.

9. Lowe, *Warren Buffett Speaks*, 111.

10. Berkshire Hathaway Annual Report, 1992.

11. Berkshire Hathaway Annual shareholders meeting, 1999.

12. "Michael Price Speaks His Mind," *Dallas Morning News*, December 15, 1996.

13. Graham, *Intelligent Investor*, 4th ed., 107.

14. Berkshire Hathaway annual shareholders meeting, 2000.

15. Lowe, *Warren Buffett Speaks*, 162.

16. Warren Buffett, Florida speech 1998 transcript.

Index

3M, 79, 82–84

A

Aaron's Sales & Lease, 59–60
ABC, 78, 86
Aflac Inc., 137
Allegheny Corporation, 58
Altria, 162
Amazon.com, 68
America Online (AOL), 66
American Express, 39, 51
American Stock Exchange (AMEX), 41
Anderson, Jeff, 47–49
Anheuser-Busch, 112
annual report, 10–13, 68–69
Anthem, Inc., 60
Apple Computer, 49, 84, 161–163
Ariel Fund, 150–151
Arrow, 111
AT&T, 163
Aviation Week, 79

B

balance sheet, 15, 16, 80, 95–100, 116

Bank of Nova Scotia, 137
Bard (C.R.), 137
Barron's, 34
Baupost Group, 28
Bear Sterns, 46, 61, 62
Bed Bath & Beyond, 79, 82–83, 137
Berkshire Hathaway, 12, 15, 16, 17, 19–20, 34, 49, 51, 53, 58, 62, 108, 147, 152, 159
BHP Billiton Ltd. ADR, 162
Biomet, 137
Bloomberg, 156
Bombay Company, 15
Boston Celtics, 36
Boston Red Sox, 14
Boston Scientific, 161–162
bottom-up approach, 8, 9–10, 18
Broadcom, 22
Brutus, 148
Buffett, Warren, 1, 4, 5, 6, 12, 17, 18, 20, 22, 26, 27, 34, 35, 36, 37–38, 39–40, 42, 50–52, 53–54, 58, 62, 65–66, 68, 70, 74–75, 76,

Buffett, Warren (*Continued*)
90, 107, 109, 110, 122,
126, 128, 130, 131, 135,
140, 141, 143, 147, 152,
155, 156, 157, 158–159,
161, 164, 165, 166, 170
Business Week, 76, 79
Butler, Bill, 59–60

C

Carnegie, Andrew, 36–37
cash flow statement, 15, 16,
100–104, 113–116
CBS, 78, 84, 86
Charles Schwab, 22
Chevron Corp., 162
Chicago Cubs, 148
Church & Dwight, 137
Churchill, Winston, 127
Cintis Corp., 137
Circuit City, 131
Cisco Systems, 64, 151–152,
162–163
Citigroup, 29, 46,
161–162
City National Corp., 137
Clipper Fund, 21
Clorox, 64
CNBC, 156
Coats, Larry Jr., 42
Coca-Cola, 9, 10, 47, 51–52,
76, 79, 82–83, 85, 87,
91–104, 108, 112, 123,
125, 130

Colgate Palmolive, 86, 137
Columbia Business School,
12, 133, 147, 156
Comcast Corp., 163
Commerce Bancshs., 137
Committee on Banking and
Commerce, 144
*Common Stocks and
Uncommon Profits*, 38
Computer Associates, 57
ConocoPhillips, 162
Constellation Brands, 112
Costco, 41
Crawford, Steve, 58
crossovers, 117
Cubic Corporation, 111
Cummings, Ian, 58
current assets and liabilities,
96–98
current ratio, 116
CVS, 68

D

Daktronics, 46
Darwin, Charles, 159
Dean Witter, 58
Dell, 46, 64, 84, 108
Delta Airlines, 111
Dentsply Int'l., 137
Devil's Dynasty, 129
DHL, 77
Disney World, 132
dividend payout ratio,
136–141

Viacom, 22, 23
Vodaphone Group ADR, 162–163

W
Walgreen Co., 68, 137
Wall Street Journal, 57, 145
Wal-Mart, 46, 61–62, 67, 126–128, 132, 137, 143
Walt Disney Co., 76
Walton, Ray, 67
Walton, Sam, 61–62, 67
Warren Buffett Portfolio, 147, 148
Washington Post, 51, 53
Waste Management, 57
WellPoint, Inc., 60
Wells Fargo, 41, 51
Wharton School, 12

Whitman, Martin, 38, 70, 109, 152
Wiley (John) & Sons, 137
Williams, John Burr, 134–135
Williams, Ted, 145
Woods, Tiger, 47
Wrigley, 86, 137

X
Xerox, 57

Y
Yacktman Fund, 149, 150–151
Yahoo!, 33, 34, 151

Z
Zimmer Holdings, 29, 162